LET'S TALK RACE, DIVERSITY, EQUITY, AND INCLUSION

by Dr. Herron Keyon Gaston

RoseDog Books

PITTSBURGH, PENNSYLVANIA 15238

RoseDog Books
585 Alpha Drive
Suite 103
Pittsburgh, PA 15238
Visit our website at www.rosedogbookstore.com

ISBN: 979-8-88527-928-4
eISBN: 979-8-88527-976-5

TABLE OF CONTENTS

PART I:
Diversity and Culture

CHAPTER 1:

What Is an Organization Culture (and Why Does it Matter?)

Organizations like to talk about their culture these days. From Twitter's rooftop meetings to Zappos' cultural fit interviews, the internet is full of companies bragging that their culture is the best—and even more posts extolling the importance of culture and insisting they have the answer for how organizations can create their own.

Unfortunately, when something becomes a buzzword it often starts to lose its meaning. More companies today are making statements about their culture than they have in the past, but it's not clear that all of them really understand what "culture" means in an organizational context. This is partially because culture is a difficult thing to define. Organizational experts agree culture exists and has a key role in influencing behavior, both as a company and as individuals who work within it, but there's less consensus about what culture actually is.

Organizational culture can broadly be defined as the observable pattern of behavior and motivations within a group or company. In an article for *Harvard Business Review*, Michael D. Watkins describes culture as a "sense-making" process that involves "creating shared awareness and understanding out of different individuals' perspectives." Put another way, an organization's culture indicates the world-view and beliefs about the workplace held by its members, as well as the beliefs its members are encouraged to act upon. Culture isn't just a definition of how members act and think, but also why they act and think the way they do. In a more informal sense, you can think of culture as the organization's personality, and it affects decision-making in the same way an individual's personality impacts their life choices.

Part of the issue with defining organizational culture is that it's not driven by a single individual or document. There are a plethora of factors that influence the real-world culture of a group, which interact in complicated and sometimes even contradictory ways. An organization trying to analyze and refine their culture is often best-served starting with these individual factors and working up toward the broader over-arching concepts that weave through and connect these disparate aspects of the group dynamic. Let's take a closer look at some of the factors that create and influence a culture.

Organization Values

Also called "core values", these are the stated guiding principles of an organization. These differ from a company policy in that they're ideas rather than actions, and are expressed in a single word or short phrase, like "diversity" or "innovation". Put another way, values are the "why" behind the "what" expressed in the organization's guidelines.

In theory, values are the basis of the culture, and will be woven into everything from the founding documents and mission statement to day-to-day decisions and interactions. It's much easier to state a value than to live it, however, and in the real world core values don't always align perfectly to on-the-ground decisions or individual behavior. In an aspirational sense, values can be seen as cultural ideals to live up to, and will be a major influence on the culture of an organization.

Individual Values

Just like an organization has its ideals for behavior, the members of it each have their own personal value system, even if they're not consciously aware of its influence over their decisions. Ideally, the values of members and the organization as a whole should align, but even within a cohesive group there will inevitably be differing points of view.

If the organizational culture is strong, it can override an individual's natural inclinations to some extent—someone doesn't have to claim "accountability" as a personal value to hold themselves and others accountable in the workplace. In a less defined culture, the personal values of leaders and major contributors have a more substantial influence over group behavior, and can end up shifting the culture to match their values, rather than the other way around.

Incentives and Discipline

An organization's policies and procedures are the practical, actionable manifestation of its values, and have a significant and direct impact on the culture. These rules spell out what will earn recognition, and what is forbidden and will result in disciplinary action.

Which behaviors are lauded (and which are punished) will influence individual behavior and the real-world organizational culture more than stated core values. Part of this is simple human nature—a reward or punishment impacts them directly, and that gives it more motivating power. Organizational procedures are also put into real-world terms that are more clearly defined than an intangible concept. Not all members may have the same interpretation of a term like "transparency", but a policy dictating that leaders share their decision-making process with employees is less open to interpretation.

Leadership and Management Style

Members look to leaders to see how they should act. Leaders are also often the main decision-makers within an organization, and the ones who enforce discipline and dole out accolades. This makes them the gatekeepers of the organization's culture, determining how policies and values are communicated to individuals and how the members are likely to behave on a day-to-day basis.

The leadership style used in an organization has a direct impact on how much agency the members get in their workplace. The more authoritarian the leadership style, the more the values of the leader will directly shape the culture of the organization. On the other end of the spectrum, servant leadership and democratic leadership styles encourage more of a group approach to culture creation since more voices are involved in decision-making.

Importance of Hierarchy

Some organizations demand adherence to proper channels of authority—think of a military branch, where communication between ranks follows a strictly-defined process. The extreme on the other end is a leaderless, anarchistic organization, something like Occupy Wall Street, which intentionally had no hierarchy and made decisions by consensus. Most organizations fall somewhere in the middle when it comes to who has the authority and how much interaction is expected between the top and bottom of the ladder.

Societal Influences

No organization exists in a vacuum. The broader societal culture in which the organization operates will inevitably have a strong influence over its goals and behavior. This can present significant challenges for multi-national or global organizations since each location will be influenced by its specific local culture, in addition to the in-organization factors outlined above.

CULTURE CREATION

Defining culture is an important first step, but it begs the question: where does culture come from? Like many things related to the topic, the answer depends largely on the organization in question, and is often more complicated than it might seem on the surface.

There are two sides to an organization's culture. One aspect is the official culture that's stated and promoted. The other is the actual culture demonstrated in decisions and actions. These would be the same thing in the perfect world, but in reality that's often not the case. Culture is fluid, and while it can be defined from the top of the hierarchy, it's also influenced by the thoughts and actions of individuals.

How do you make sure your "walk" matches your "talk" when it comes to culture? The first step is understanding the ways culture forms within a group and the differences between an intentional culture and one that forms organically.

Intentional Culture

An intentional culture is just like it sounds: a pattern of cohesive behavior originating from the top that's disseminated through the organization's leadership. These, in turn, shape the behavior, thought process, and perceptions of individuals, who internalize this culture and use it to guide their actions and decisions while they're in the group context.

Groups that have an intentional culture don't just create the culture then step back and call it done. It has to be continuously monitored and reinforced at every level of the organization. When the culture starts to veer from its intended path, leaders step in to correct it. Individuals can also be empowered to be "culture watchdogs" in organizations with a strong culture, using the power of peer pressure to bring members who are out of step with the culture back in line.

Some of the most useful tools in creating an intentional culture include:

- **Selective recruiting.** When leaders are given a clear definition of the culture, they can choose new members who fit those standards. New members who share the organization's values will be more likely to reinforce the existing culture, rather than acting in opposition to it.

- **Onboarding and training.** An organic culture often needs to be felt and experienced to be understood, but an intentional culture can be taught. A cultural aspect during onboarding ensures new members are aware of the expectations, and can provide an additional layer of screening for individuals who don't share these values.

- **Recognition.** Rewarding those who exemplify the culture demonstrates an organizational commitment to those values. It also serves as a visible example to other members of what ideal cultural behavior looks like, giving them a target to aim toward as they adjust their behavior to match.

- **Communication.** The content of communications is obviously important, but how that information is conveyed also reinforces the culture. Language choices, tone, and the level of formality of official communications all convey culture to the reader. The preferred method of communication can make a difference here, too. Culture is different in an all-remote workplace that communicates virtually than one based in a small office where information is mostly conveyed in face-to-face conversation.

- **Key metrics.** The criteria used to evaluate members indicates what the organization considers to be important, so leaders should choose metrics that reinforce the core values. If you want an innovative culture, for example, members should be praised rather than penalized for taking risks.

- **Feedback and disagreements.** Just like communication, both the content and method matter here. An organization that values transparency will be more likely to allow open feedback and group debate when there's a disagreement, while others prefer to send feedback along established hierarchy channels and handle disputes behind closed doors.

Organic Culture

The best way to see organic culture in action is to think about your main group of friends. You probably have a certain way you talk when you're together, and certain shared interests or favorite activities that tend to influence what you do when you hang out. Nobody wrote down rules that made things this way. You all, collectively and unconsciously, came to these decisions, and those patterns of behavior were reinforced through repetition.

This is how the culture forms in many small organizations, especially small businesses and grassroots groups that began as just a few people and grew over time. An organic culture isn't inherently bad. The issue for organizations is that organic cultures are unpredictable and unstable. They rely on the influence of individuals to shape them. If those individuals change, the culture changes with it, and not always in a way that benefits the organization as a whole.

Some form of organic culture will naturally exist between any group of people, and is healthy in an organization. It enhances the feeling of belonging when individuals are allowed to have some input into how the group interacts. The question leaders need to answer is which aspects of the culture need to stay consistent and which can be allowed to naturally develop, and this isn't always cut and dry. An informal tradition of going to a certain bar for workplace celebrations might seem innocuous, for example, but a culture of celebratory drinking could be exclusionary for those in recovery, or adherents of certain religions. On the other hand, demanding that members obtain leadership approval for every workplace celebration can lead to a sterile feeling that pushes individuals away rather than making them feel included. In the end, it's a matter of balance, and finding that balance can be an ongoing process.

WHY CULTURE MATTERS

Culture has broad implications for an organization—and that's part of the problem with identifying its impact. It's an inextricable factor in every leadership decision and coworker interaction. This broad scope is one of the biggest challenges for organizations trying to identify and address issues.

In an organization with a strong culture, members know how they're expected to respond to any given situation and believe they'll be rewarded for doing so, even if that's not the way they'd typically act if left to their own devices. This consistency gives the organization a defined identity that can be seen from both outside and within. Once you have this strong culture, it becomes a kind of self-controlling system. Since the organization's identity is clear, it will naturally draw those individuals who identify similarly, who will reinforce these values and strengthen the culture further; since the individual members are more likely to align, there's an implicit shared understanding of what's important and valuable to the collective, and less chance of shifts or discrepancies in the core values of individuals.

The specific benefits of a strong culture are numerous, but some of the most valuable include:

- Decisions can be made more efficiently since every member has a clear idea of the goals and values that should influence group decisions.
- Stronger trust bonds within the organization form when members can expect each other to act within the behavioral standards of the culture.
- Sharing ideas and collaboration is easier since there's a universal framework for communication.
- Team members understand their expectations and are enabled to contribute, which leads to higher engagement and lower turnover.
- Shared ideals and goals leads to fewer conflicts between members, and more productive resolution of them when they do occur.

The bottom line is that a strong cultural framework indicates the proper way to behave within the organization, and that can prevent or limit a multitude of common issues, both organizational and interpersonal. A strong culture is the common thread that links successful organizations, from global corporations to volunteer community groups.

Impacts of a Weak Culture

The benefits of a strong culture are clear—but does that mean an organization with a weak culture is doomed to fail? The short answer is not necessarily. An absence of a defined culture doesn't automatically doom you to have a toxic work environment that kills member engagement and leads to high turnover. An organic culture will develop to fill in the gap, and if the values of leaders and members match with the organization's as a whole, this organic culture can still look and feel very close to the ideal.

The issue, of course, comes down to that "if". An organization that doesn't define its own culture is banking on having committed, like-minded people in positions of authority. In most groups, the culture of the leader will become the culture of the collective if there's not a consistent standard everyone is working toward. This often happens with start-ups and other small businesses. The founder's personality becomes the company culture, and if that founder leaves there's often a void where the group's identity used to be.

A strong culture gives members a foundation for making decisions and responding to new situations. Without this, they'll default to their personal value system. Again, if the values of members align with those of the organization, there may not be much of a visible difference, but this will come down to the individual—a "me"-centered approach, rather than the "we"-centric attitude developed by a consistent and well-communicated intentional culture, where the needs of the organization take precedence by default.

CULTURE AS PROCESS, NOT ARTIFACT

Think back to the "you" you were as a teenager. The things you considered important, the ones that influenced most of your decisions, were probably a bit different then than they are now. Your core identity is the same, but your definition of yourself has been refined over the years. This doesn't mean the teenage version of you was wrong; that iteration of yourself was necessary to build the person that you are today. If you used those same criteria for your decisions as an adult, however, that could lead to some problems. You've picked up knowledge and experience as you've matured that has shifted your identity and goals, creating a new (hopefully better) personality.

The same thing is true of the culture in organizations. Ideal culture isn't a set destination that you can arrive at to reach organizational utopia. Just like individual identity, group identity shifts over time in response to new knowledge and ideas. If the culture doesn't evolve with it, you'll be the metaphorical adult making decisions based on a teenager's value system.

Like individual personalities, culture is fluid and dynamic, always shifting in response to new knowledge, driven by both internal and external factors. Rather than trying to wrangle this into a static, unchanging thing, view it as a process of continuous improvement and development. The same thing goes when you're trying to analyze your culture. Don't waste too much time and energy trying to pin down a moving target, but embrace culture as a process that must be continuously managed and refined.

In a similar vein, it's helpful to remember that the culture doesn't need to be a monolith, especially in larger organizations. In a group of a dozen people, a single main culture can probably encompass all of them. But for a global corporation with a dozen locations, it's unrealistic to expect every office to maintain the same day-to-day traditions and work environment—and, actually, that's probably not want you even want. Part of the value of a diverse workforce is access to a variety of worldviews and perspectives, and that can be squelched if you try to impose a blanket mono-culture from top to bottom.

Most healthy large organizations have a main culture, disseminated from the center and top, that serves as the basis of the various subcultures that exist in different locations, departments, or teams within it. Refining culture in these situations is a matter of deciding which aspects are crucial to the organization's identity and ensuring those remain consistent across subcultures. Like most aspects of culture, this isn't an exact science and there's no one-size-fits-all approach that will work for every organization. Once you're aware of how a culture is formed and its implications for your team, you can find the strategy that best fits your identity.

CHAPTER 2:

What Exactly Is Unconscious Bias?

Most people don't want to be racist. While there are exceptions, the majority of people believe everyone should be treated equally, and that it's wrong to discriminate against someone because of the color of their skin. While this is a good thing, it does have a flip side. The more people believe racism is wrong, the more upset they're likely to get when confronted about discriminatory actions or speech—especially if they're already self-conscious of biases they've been working internally to un-do.

This is why it's important to bring more nuance to discussions about race. Many instances of discrimination are unintentional. The offending individual often isn't working to discriminate against people of color. In fact, they may actively be trying to support equality in their organization, but have a blind spot for certain types of biased behavior. When discrimination is presented as a binary, where "bias" and "racist" are seen as synonyms, it's more likely to trigger a defensive reaction because the call-out perceived as an attack on the individual, not a critique of the behavior. Conversely, acknowledging that well-meaning people can still have biases that influence their words and actions smooths the path for deeper conversations and meaningful change. With that in mind, let's dig a bit deeper into what bias actually is and where it comes from.

HOW BIASES FORM

In our day-to-day life, the human brain is bombarded with an extraordinary amount of information. To make sense of all that information, it uses past experiences as a kind of template for what to do when those things are encountered in the future. This can be very helpful in a survival sense—it's how we know a sour smell means we shouldn't drink that milk, or that we should duck when someone shouts "head's up!".

The problem is, the brain doesn't always form these templates from complete information. If the first peach you ever eat is hard and underripe, you might decide you don't like peaches and avoid buying them in the future. Your brain is just trying to help you eat things you like, but it's made an unfair assumption. Peaches might be your favorite fruit—but you'll never know if you don't stop to think about why you feel the way you do.

This becomes even more complicated when it comes to interpersonal interactions, mostly because humans themselves are incredibly complex. Even identical twins have their own personality. The opinions and behavior of one individual are never accurate predictors of others who share physical traits. But while most of us know this on a conscious level, the part of our brain that forms these thought templates doesn't operate consciously. It's programmed to simplify the equation for the purpose of making split-second decisions, and if you don't slow down and analyze your own thought processes, you may not even be aware how these simplified "X=Y" associations are impacting your decision making.

These unconsciously-formed thought patterns are the basis of unintentional bias. If you're reading this wondering if you have these biases, the answer is probably yes—and you're not alone. A 1998 study conducted by social psychologists from Yale University and the University of Washington found that 90-95% of study participants have implicit biases.

This doesn't mean more than 90% of people are racist. In a 2020 poll by Monmouth University, 76% of Americans surveyed felt racial discrimination is a serious problem in the United States that needs to be addressed. Just by looking at these numbers, it's obvious that many of the people who feel that way still have unconscious biases even though, in their conscious mind, they firmly believe that it's wrong to discriminate based on someone's appearance.

So how do they still have biases? Doesn't that contradict their belief system? If the bias is examined, yes, and this is how unconscious biases are ultimately torn down. Remember, though, these assumptions happen instantaneously, before reaching your conscious mind. These thought templates are your brain's version of auto-pilot: they come into play when you're *not* paying attention. Unless you slow down and observe your thought process in action, you may not even notice the ways they're steering you off course.

Internalized Oppression

There is no better example of how insidious unconscious bias can be than the phenomenon of internalized oppression or self-oppression. For those unfamiliar with the term, this is when an individual from an oppressed group incorporates the stereotypes and biases of their oppressors into their self-image. These beliefs can very often become a self-fulfilling prophecy: for example, a woman who internalizes that she's too emotional to lead may avoid putting herself forward for promotions into leadership positions, never getting the experience that would have revealed her true leadership potential.

When an oppressed individual internalizes the oppressor's worldview, it often makes them feel as though they're inherently less capable than those from different groups. They may see that they're being treated differently but don't view that as unfair because they see themselves as having less value. This is obviously very damaging to an individual's self-esteem and mental health, and can have wider-reaching societal consequences, too.

A historical example of the societal impact of self-oppression is the phenomenon of colorism. The internalized association of "light" with "good" led to discrimination against those with darker skin tones within the black community; many with darker skin felt compelled to use make-up or cosmetic surgery to lighten their tone because they had bought-in to the idea that lighter skin was more attractive.

It's important to note that not every member of an oppressed group internalizes that oppression. Like all biases, it all comes down to the individual and their internal thoughts, something nobody can see from the outside. What it does mean is that no one is immune from biases. You can't assume the white men in your organization are the only ones to blame for a lack of diversity, or that people of color won't benefit from diversity training. Remember, a positive stereotype is still a stereotype. Thinking someone can't have biases because they're black is as problematic as any other assumption based on race.

BIAS, PREJUDICE, AND RACISM: WHAT'S THE DIFFERENCE?

By its dictionary definition, "discrimination" is not inherently negative; it's a synonym of "discernment": the ability to differentiate between two things. There's nothing wrong with having discriminating taste in, say, sports cars or craft beer—just like with implicit biases, it becomes a problem when you start applying it to other people. When someone says they're against discrimination, they're using the term as a shorthand for a more specific concept, what could be more accurately called "social discrimination."

This may seem slightly pedantic, but if you want to bring nuance into a conversation, you need a more nuanced vocabulary around the concept. Many of the terms used to talk about race have become loaded to the point their meaning is muddled. Racism, prejudice, and bias are not exact synonyms, though they're often used like they are. Understanding the differences between them can go a long way toward finding the best approach to identifying and eliminating them.

A bias can be broadly described as a feeling in favor or against something. Prejudice is a subcategory of bias, and applies specifically to a negative view, with the implication it's an opinion based on hearsay or assumptions rather than lived experience. When a bias based on an oversimplification or misunderstanding becomes widespread, it becomes a stereotype. If this stereotype is based on skin color, it is racism, which can be loosely defined as believing specific races possess intrinsic characteristics or abilities that make them superior or inferior to others. A person who has consciously embraced this belief is racist.

That element of conscious choice is key to pinpointing the difference between unconscious bias and overt racism. To put it in the words of Prejudice Lab director Patricia Devine: "Neural connections aren't moral. What people do with them is." Having a bias doesn't make someone a bad person—it makes them normal. This doesn't mean you should just accept your biases and go about your day, any more than you should accept any bad habit. But acknowledging the distinction makes conversations about race productive by keeping the focus on the bias, not the person holding it.

Structural Biases

Personal biases come from what you might call "the back of your brain." They were constructed at some point in your past, maybe as far back as childhood; you may not even remember the experience or information that led to its creation. The same thing can happen within an organization's culture over time. The worldview of the members, especially the leadership, becomes baked into the policies, traditions, and behavior that make up the culture, and sticks around even after those individuals leave the group.

A structural bias can be defined as any institutionalized practice that gives advantages to certain individuals based on their identity or physical characteristics, rather than relevant skills, knowledge, or experience. Just like with personal biases, these are so worked into the day-to-day decision making process that even those within the affected group may not be aware of the ways in which they're unfair and the harm they're causing.

Since it's often impossible to determine the intent behind long-held company policies and traditions, rooting out these biases can be difficult. Sometimes they may seem logical and unbiased on the surface and the problems become apparent only when you dig deeper. A hiring policy that focuses on applicants who are a good "cultural fit" may on the surface seem like a good idea for the group's cohesion until you look more closely and interrogate the traits that are considered to make someone a good fit.

Another problem with removing structural biases is that they often become enshrined as tradition, and that makes it more difficult to change. An easy example to consider is the Washington Redskins. Even more so than other problematic sports team names, "redskin" is an overtly racist term. But many fans of the team, even those who oppose racism and would never use slurs in their speech, resisted changing the name. It was part of the team's history, they argued, and that history carried more weight in the minds of fans than the potential harm of having a racist term as a team moniker for many years. The same thing can happen on a smaller scale within an organization. Even obviously discriminatory or racist policies can stick around far longer than one might expect out of members' desire to respect the past.

IDENTIFYING UNCONSCIOUS BIAS

If many people can't even see their own biases, how can you tell if other people have them? The short answer is, you really can't. All you can judge is how you perceive another person's words or actions, and that's not always going to be accurate. This makes identifying bias a collaborative process, in many cases. Only the individual can say for sure why they make the choices they do, but they may need help from an outside perspective to notice the biases they're blind to.

To identify your own implicit bias involves a process known as meta-cognition, or thinking about how you think. This isn't something most of us do as a matter of course, but it's something anyone can do with a bit of practice. After you make a decision, stop for a second and consider what steps you just took to reach that conclusion, examining all the factors that went into it and where that knowledge came from. If there's a factor in there whose provenance you can't identify, dig deeper and investigate where that thought originated. This can be a tedious process at first, but will become more natural the more you do it.

Identifying biases in other people or structural biases within organizations can be a more fraught process. The perception of bias is not a guarantee that it exists—for all you know, your own biases are coloring your interpretation of the situation—but it is a valid feeling, and shouldn't be ignored. The difficulty comes in voicing those feelings without it feeling like an attack on the other person, which will send them naturally into defense mode. A person who's in a defensive mindset is the least able to analyze and change their own thoughts. This is something else that's baked into our brains by evolution. Defensive feelings trigger similar fight-or-flight physiological responses as the threat of physical danger, telling the brain it should be prepared to make fast survival decisions. As a result, someone who is feeling defensive more likely to rely on established thought patterns. When you think you see a colleague saying or doing something biased, it's better to ask questions than make accusations. Asking "How did you arrive at that decision?" encourages the person to interrogate their thought process instead of going into defensive mode.

Knowing the right words to identify the type of bias you're detecting can also help, both with self-analysis and with directing conversations with colleagues. Some of the common forms of bias you may come across include:

- **Affinity bias**: A favorable view toward those who have similar interests, experiences, or other traits to one's own.
- **Anchoring bias**: Giving undue weight to the first piece of information received, and basing judgments about future information off of this information anchor rather than considering each piece of knowledge objectively.
- **Availability bias**: Giving undue weight to information that can be quickly recalled, even if that's not the best representation of the concept.
- **The Barnum Effect**: Filling in gaps in your knowledge with what you think makes sense, or paying attention to the

information you think is useful while discarding the rest, even if your judgment of this is flawed.

- **Confirmation bias**: Seeking out or giving extra weight to information that aligns with your existing beliefs, while giving less weight to information that contradicts them.

- **Declinism**: Favoring the past over the present because of a skewed perception of this past that ignores improvements or gains in the present while focusing on what used to be better.

- **The Dunning-Kruger Effect:** Perceiving a concept to be simple because your understanding of that concept is lacking, and assuming you understand a concept fully because your lack of in-depth knowledge prevents you from perceiving the concept's true complexity.

- **Fundamental Attribution Error**: Attributing an individual's behavior to stereotypes based on their identity or physical traits.

- **The Halo Effect**: Focusing on one positive trait to the extent it blinds you to the existence of negative traits.

- **The Horns Effect**: The opposite of the Halo Effect, this is focusing on a single poorly-perceived trait, clouding perception of potential positives.

- **In-group bias**: The tendency to favor those within a social group over outsiders, or apply a different set of standards to people one knows personally than the general population (e.g. if your friend is late you assume it was out of their control; if a stranger is late, you assume they're lazy).

- **Name bias**: Making assumptions about an individual based on their name. This is most often cited with first names, especially discrimination against foreign-sounding or "African" names, though it can also apply to family names and reputations (e.g.

expecting the son of a business founder to share their parent's leadership style and skills because they share a last name).

- **Status quo bias**: The desire to keep things in their current state and tendency to see any change as a negative, regardless of the actual impact of said change.

The Problem with Color Blindness

The phrase "I don't see color" sounds good on the surface. After all, isn't that the ultimate goal—to create an environment where everyone gets the same respect and opportunities and their skin color doesn't matter?

The problem is, this simply isn't true. Unless the person saying this has a visual impairment, they absolutely do see the difference between skin tones. What they're actually saying is they believe they make absolutely zero assumptions about a person based on that information. This firm belief that they're "all good" prevents them from doing the kind of introspection necessary to identify biases that have taken root in their psyche. An unconscious bias is a thought habit that needs to be broken, and doing so means first acknowledging that the habit exists. Claiming color blindness is actively refusing awareness of these habits, and that guarantees they'll never change.

Even if that individual truly doesn't have any unconscious biases, the odds are high the same can't be said for the people and organizations they interact with. Failing to acknowledge skin color as a potential cause of discrimination makes you blind to instances of bias happening around you. A leader with a "color blind" mindset can end up perpetuating structural biases in their organization because their narrowed view isn't tuned in to race as a possible cause of discrimination.

A study by Coqual, an anti-bias think tank, found that 2/3 of the employees of color they interviewed were uncomfortable talking about race relations in the workplace. Nearly 1/3 (29%) felt it is never acceptable to discuss race at their company. This compounds the problem of color blindness in white would-be allies. For one thing, it leads to a perception that bias doesn't exist because the white individual doesn't hear about it, reinforcing their belief that they are free of any race-based misconceptions. It also makes those who claim color blindness a more significant problem. If they don't feel the need to discuss race, they can't help to create an environment where those who are affected by discrimination feel empowered to share their experiences.

THE POWER OF PERCEPTION

Remember the dress meme? Here's a refresher: a picture went around the internet of a blue-and-black striped dress that many people were convinced was actually white and gold. The cause, as scientists would later explain, was the brain's tendency to make assumptions. These people saw the blue and black hues, but their brain interpreted those as a lighter dress cast in shadow—and, once their brain decided that's what they were seeing, they couldn't see it any other way.

Bias is like this. You can be convinced that what you're seeing is correct, even if you're absolutely wrong. Our brains fill in gaps in our knowledge faster than we're aware of it happening. Exactly what it fills into those gaps and how you perceive your reality depends on your values, experiences, background, and world-view.

Individuals who are in the majority are less likely to perceive instances of bias than those in a minority group who are more likely to be affected by it. Enabling these groups to share their differing perspectives is the only way to identify and eliminate biases, both in individuals and system bias worked into an organization. The more aware someone is of the existence of bias, the more likely they'll be to identify it when they see it happening around them.

CHAPTER 3:

Why Is Diversity a Good Thing?

It's become a widely-accepted fact that diversity is a good thing, but even people who believe this strongly might have some trouble clarifying exactly why. For many, it's a moral imperative, particularly in places like the United States that have a multi-cultural population. If everyone is getting access to the same opportunities, the typical membership and leadership of businesses, schools, and other organizations should reflect this. Increasing diversity opens more opportunities for a wider range of people.

Unfortunately, it's often difficult to convince organization leaders to spend money on initiatives just to "do the right thing." Arguments based on moral premises also won't carry much water with individuals who have differing belief systems. For these situations, you need provable facts to present if you want to have any hope of changing minds and gaining support for your ideas. With that in mind, let's take a look at some of the main practical benefits and advantages that come along with having a more varied team.

BENEFIT #1: INCREASED CREATIVITY AND INNOVATION.

Innovation happens when new solutions are applied to familiar problems. Companies today have a lot of approaches to fostering a culture of innovation, often focusing on the work environment or encouraging existing team members to collaborate or think about things from new angles. While these kinds of adjustments can help bring out more creativity from team members, the diversity of the members is a big factor in how innovative a team has the capacity to be.

Every member of a team brings a unique set of skills and experiences to the table, but just how unique each set is depends on the make-up of the group. In a team made entirely of thirty-something white Midwesterners, individual members likely have similar educational experiences, cultural traditions, values, and belief systems—they may not be identical, but they fall within a narrow arc of the full spectrum. Because they share much of their worldview, the individuals on the team are likely to approach problems in a similar way and come to similar conclusions about the best solution. This is great for building quick consensus, but doesn't promote the kind of debate that opens up new paths so while homogenous teams can still innovate, they're more likely to reinforce the status quo.

A diverse team brings more worldviews to the table, and this gives the collective a broader perspective. In brainstorming sessions, these disparate ideas can challenge and influence each other, taking the conversation in a different direction than either idea would have led to on its own. Members of the team also learn from each other as they interact, acquiring new skills and considering fresh ideas that build toward more innovations in the future.

BENEFIT #2: BETTER AGILITY AND PROBLEM-SOLVING CAPABILITY.

In a two-year study of 450 global companies conducted by the Josh Bersin Academy, the companies that were the most inclusive were also 1.8 times more change-ready than those that lacked diversity. A 2017 whitepaper from the management software developer Cloverpop had similar findings. Their study of 600 businesses found that those with a diverse team of decision-makers outperformed individual decision-makers 87% of the time.

It seems counter-intuitive—one would think a homogenous team or individual leader could make faster decisions and be more agile. While a single person might have a speed advantage that doesn't mean they're making the best choice. The broader perspective of a diverse team means they can see more potential solutions at the same time and approach the problem from multiple angles simultaneously. This ultimately results in faster, better solutions for new or complex problems.

The range of skillsets in a diverse team can also help an organization stay change-ready. If your team comes from a variety of backgrounds, it's more likely one of them will know a tool or strategy that can help solve whatever challenge you're facing. This saves time in both the planning and implementation of new strategies, business pivots, and other changes, a big reason more diverse companies are also more adaptable.

BENEFIT #3: HIGHER PRODUCTIVITY AND PROFITS.

Diversity is good for business, and there's data to prove it. In that Josh Bersin study mentioned above, inclusive companies had a per-employee cash flow roughly 2.3 times higher than that of companies lacking diversity over the 3-year span they analyzed. Research from international consulting firm McKinsey & Company found a direct correlation between diversity and financial growth among public companies in North America and the United Kingdom, showing those that were ethnically diverse were 35% more likely to see financial returns above the national median for their industry.

The why behind this is a bit harder to pin down. It's in part thanks to that same variety of skillsets that make a company more agile. As team members collaborate, they learn these skills for each other, giving everyone on the team a larger toolkit to draw from when they're going about their tasks. More cognitive diversity also improves your ability to spot new markets or opportunities that could be in the blind spot of a more homogenous team, and gives you the capability to take advantage of them when you do. This, too, is backed by data. A study by Boston Consulting Group found that companies with above-average diversity saw a bigger payoff from innovation and higher margins on their earnings overall than those with below-average rankings.

Another big factor in play here is employee engagement. Employees who feel respected and valued are more likely to feel invested in their workplace and create bonds of trust and loyalty with both their coworkers and their employer. This, in turn, means they'll put more energy into their work and perform at a higher level on average. A diverse workplace encourages higher engagement because it creates an environment where more employees feel included. In a homogenous workplace, those who have differing opinions often don't feel comfortable sharing them, or think they won't be taken seriously if they do. When the workplace is diverse there isn't this kind of clear-cut majority, and that creates an environment where everyone can have a valuable role.

BENEFIT #4: YOU'LL RECRUIT BETTER PEOPLE.

The data from the 2020 census shows that the United States is more multi-cultural than ever. People of color represent 43% of the country's population today, an increase of almost 10% over the 2010 census figures. If your organization isn't attracting a diverse group of people, you're missing nearly half of the available population—and all of the unique skills they could have brought to the table.

Diversity is also more important for the average American than it's ever been in the past. According to the job search site Glassdoor, more than 2/3 of job seekers say diversity is an important factor when they're deciding whether to work for a company. In this same survey, 37% said they wouldn't apply for a job with a company whose employee satisfaction rates differed between racial groups.

The bottom line is, encouraging diversity in your recruitment efforts lets you attract the people who will best support your goals, no matter what they look like. People want to see that they have a future with an organization before they commit their energy to it. Potential members from all backgrounds will be more likely to join your team if they see it as a place where they can thrive.

BENEFIT #5: BETTER BRAND REPUTATION AND MARKET POSITIONING.

Job seekers aren't the only people who care about diversity. Consumers are increasingly socially conscious and want to spend their money with companies that support their values, and inclusivity is one of the top values of interest for many. Companies that promote diversity arc on the whole seen as more socially responsible and friendlier. That said, the internet makes it easier than ever for customers to find out if companies promoting diversity actually practice what they preach, with a plethora of platforms to call out any that fail to live up to thcir standards.

This can create a tricky situation for organizations. Take, for example, diversity in advertising. According to a 2019 research report by Adobe, 61% of Americans think diversity in advertising is important. In that same survey, 66% of Black respondents and 53% of Latino respondents said portrayals of their race in advertisements were often stereotypical. The companies that made these ads probably meant well, but their attempts to increase diversity ended up coming across as insensitive or offensive. The negative impacts of this can range from losing trust of customers in those market segments to media call-outs, boycotts, and other blights on the company's reputation.

Increasing diversity can help organizations avoid these kinds of reputation-killing snafus. When multiple ethnicities are represented and have a voice in business decisions, the team's less likely to make cultural blunders or play into unconscious biases that lead to unintentionally offensive statements and portrayals. It also adds a layer of authenticity to public statements about diversity, or ad campaigns targeted at specific demographic groups, making you a brand that more people will trust.

Having a diverse team can also help your organization reach new groups of people—or, in business terms, to expand your market segment. Someone who belongs to a community understands their needs and values better than someone who doesn't, and can share those insights with the rest of the team. A team with varied backgrounds has this kind of "inside scoop" on a wider range of groups than one whose members are all from one community.

BENEFIT #6: BETTER MORALE AND RETENTION.

In the year of the Great Resignation, employee retention is a hot button issue. While losing staff is a particularly costly problem for businesses, the truth is losing members isn't good for any kind of organization, leading to instability, loss of knowledge, and increased stress for those who are left carrying the workload.

There is a direct correlation between high engagement and high retention. It's a common sense statement, when you think about it: people are more likely to keep contributing to a team when they feel like a valued member. Many of the same factors that go into an inclusive environment are also key for improving engagement, like increased transparency, leadership empathy, and mutual respect between members.

Conversely, if someone feels like they don't fit in and are always being over-ruled, it's no surprise if they decide to leave. Lack of diversity in an organization creates an environment that's unintentionally hostile to those who don't fit the mold, one where they don't feel comfortable speaking up about biases they perceive or sharing opinions that go against the majority. Not only does this make them more likely to quit, but it also hinders your ability to improve the environment for future members.

BENEFIT #7: REDUCED ORGANIZATIONAL BIAS.

One of the main ways biases and stereotypes take root is because people don't have enough real-world experience with people from different backgrounds, ethnicities, or cultures to realize the error in their assumptions. Regularly interacting with a diverse array of people expands an individual's worldview, helping them identify and deconstruct their own unconscious biases, and making them more observant of biases in the world around them.

The same is true of structural biases within organizations. A diverse group will be able to spot and eliminate biases that have been written into the processes or bylaws better than one that's more homogenous. This creates a kind of snowball effect. Increasing diversity helps to break down barriers to further inclusivity that exist in both the organization as a whole and the individual members that belong to it. This, in turn, creates an even more inclusive atmosphere.

THE IMPORTANCE OF A DIVERSE LEADERSHIP

All of these potential benefits we've discussed in this chapter can result from having a more diverse organization overall. While that's a great first step, a truly inclusive organization is diverse at every level, from the upper leadership down to the newest recruits, and achieving this kind of sweeping diversity has its own unique benefits.

For one thing, a diverse leadership makes it much easier to attract and retain a diverse overall team. When a variety of worldviews are present in upper leadership, individual members are more likely to have someone they can relate to. This builds trust and makes the organization feel more welcoming and safer for both new and existing members. In turn, this also encourages team members to be more forthcoming with their feedback or insights since they're more likely to feel like someone in leadership will support them. In this way, diverse leadership can also be a catalyst of greater innovation and creativity across hierarchy levels. Findings from the Josh Bersin/Deloitte study back up this claim. In their research, companies with diverse leadership levels were about 4 times as likely to effectively coach employees to improve their performance, and 3 times as likely to effectively build new leaders within the company. They also showed greater ability to deal with personnel and performance problems effectively compared to less diverse leadership teams.

This welcoming of new ideas has other benefits, too, similar to what happens with the team as a whole. More perspectives in the decision-making process allows the team to make faster and more informed decisions, with fewer blind spots to potential solutions. Having a variety of experiences to draw from among the organization's primary decision makers gives the entire team a broader outlook, making them more innovative, more agile, and better able to navigate fast-changing or complex situations for the best results.

The best news for business leaders is that a more diverse leadership team makes the company more profitable, and this is especially true when it comes to racial and ethnic diversity. Studies show global corporations with ethnically diverse executive branches are 30% more profitable on average. Among companies in the United States, those that increased diversity over the study period saw a boost in earnings, with a 10% increase in diversity equating to a 1% increase in profits on average.

Many organizations that are looking to increase their diversity start from the member level, with the thought this will eventually work its way up to leadership. When you look at the data, however, it's clear increasing diversity at the leadership level has the most significant impact on the organization, and is much more likely to trickle down through the team than the other way around.

THE BOTTOM LINE ON DIVERSITY

One difficulty with getting buy-in for programs to improve diversity is that, while most people feel diversity as a concept is a good thing, it can be difficult to quantify and demonstrate its tangible benefits. But as you can see from the studies and figures rounded up in this chapter, increasing diversity isn't just a feel-good moral decision—it's a smart business move that can substantially improve an organization's competitiveness, adaptability, and overall productivity.

As a last note, it's important to keep in mind that diversity isn't just a black-and-white issue. One of the largest diversity surveys we reviewed was conducted by *Harvard Business Review* in 2013, and surveyed 1,800 professionals along with including data from dozens of case studies, focus groups, and interviews across industries. They identified two types of diversity: one based on inherent traits (such as race or gender) and one based on acquired traits based on experiences, such as religious beliefs, cultural traditions, or languages spoken. In their research, the organizations that exhibited at least 3 inherent and 3 acquired traits in their leadership team, what they call "2-D diversity", out-performed the others by a wide margin.

The bottom line is that an organization with a truly inclusive environment will see the most direct benefits associated with increased diversity. Too often, organizations bring on a few token minorities then go about business as usual and wonder why they're not seeing boosts to innovation and engagement. This kind of band-aid fix doesn't address the problems that prevented people of color, women, or other minorities from thriving in the first place. So what are those barriers, and why do so many organizations struggle to overcome them? We'll tackle those questions in the next section.

PART II:
Impacts of Bias
(and Why It's So Hard to Eliminate)

CHAPTER 4:

Does Race Really Matter?

Lab tests and studies can target specific variables and set up control groups to reach definite conclusions. In the real world, things are rarely so clear-cut; nothing exists in a vacuum, and it's much more difficult (if not impossible) to isolate causes, effects, and influences. Individual perception compounds this problem. What one person sees as race-based discrimination another could perceive as a judgment made on performance, ability, or cultural fit. They're looking at the same situation but from different angles. Not only is there no solid way to prove which view is the right one, there's the chance that both are correct to some extent—and, even then, the question is focused only on the present, ignoring the added complexities of how race affects the individual's life path in a broader sense.

This nuance makes it difficult to demonstrate how race affects a person's opportunities and experiences. For those who have experienced discrimination, race obviously matters and there's no need to prove it. Those who haven't can't fully comprehend that experience, no matter how many times it's described or explained to them. Luckily, a plethora of studies have been conducted over the past 50 years that help to frame systemic racism in a way that can be understood by those who aren't directly affected by it. In this chapter, we'll focus primarily on the ways in which race impacts an individual's path to joining an organization, and how they're able to contribute and advance within it.

GENERATIONAL WEALTH

For the purposes of this chapter, wealth can be generally described as the assets an individual or family owns above their debts and baseline living expenses. The generation of wealth is a crucial part of economic mobility and financial freedom. In the present, it serves as a safety net when things go awry, whether it's a personal crisis like an illness or injury or a wide-spread emergency like a natural disaster or pandemic. Over time, wealth generates income through interest and appreciation, creating a snowball effect, and can be passed down along family lines to afford the next generation the same stability and future income potential.

In 2016, the median wealth of a white family in the United States was $171,000. The median wealth of a black family was $17,150—roughly 10% the wealth of the median white family. This is not an area where equality is growing, either. The ratio of white to black wealth is wider now than it was at the start of the century. Home ownership is one of the most reliable ways for a family to build wealth, providing stability that makes it easier to plan for the future along with the value of the property itself, and home ownership rates in the United States show an equally stark disparity along racial lines. In 2017, about 43% of black Americans owned a home, down from around 50% in 2004 and lower than the rates for white Americans (73%), Asian Americans (56%), Native Americans (50%), and Hispanic Americans (46%).

Much of this disparity is rooted in history. Jim Crow laws endured in many states for a hundred years after the abolishment of slavery, limiting business opportunities, particularly in southern states. Those black entrepreneurs who overcame these limitations often faced violent opposition, like the massacre in Tulsa's Greenwood District, while segregation limited the resources, properties, and institutions that black Americans could access. The combined effect of these racist laws and actions was to prevent the accumulation of wealth in the black community before it had a chance to grow. Since wealth begets wealth, the gap has continued to widen between white and black Americans over the years, despite cultural shifts ending the policies that created the problem.

Because of this, black Americans who do acquire wealth are more likely to be called upon to help neighbors, family, and their community, rather than being able to invest their spare income for their own future. The practice of redlining, or denying loans and other financial resources to residents of certain neighborhoods, further impairs this wealth growth, leading to under-valuation of the homes within that area. In metro areas across the United States, homes in neighborhoods that are predominantly black (50% of residents or more) are valued at about half the price of homes in predominantly white neighborhoods. These price differences can't be rationalized by differences in neighborhood amenities, crime rates, home age and maintenance, or other commonly-cited excuses. Direct comparisons of homes that are similar on these criteria show homes in majority-black neighborhoods are worth 23% less on average than those in majority-white neighborhoods, an undervaluation of $48,000 per home on average, amounting to more than $150 billion in cumulative losses for homeowners in these communities. These disparities are highest in metro areas that are the most racially segregated.

What does all of this have to do with race in organizations? The short answer is that where and how you grow up has a huge impact on the education and experiences in your formative years, and that has implications that reach far into the future. For the longer answer, let's break things down a bit more granularly.

K-12 Education

In the United States, public schools often receive most of their funding from taxes on properties in their district. Since property tax rates are determined as a percentage of the home's value, undervaluation automatically reduces the amount of funding available to schools in those communities. This has led to the U.S. education system being one of the most unequal in the developed world, with the wealthiest 10% of school districts spending about 10 times as much money per student as the poorest 10%. Just like with generational wealth, this lack of funding compounds over time. Families with means either move to a better-funded district or send their kids to private schools, creating unequal access to education based on economic class.

Equal access to opportunities has a demonstrably positive effect on educational outcomes. After the end of legal segregation in the U.S. in 1964, the gap between standardized test scores for white and minority students decreased substantially. The most marked improvement was to average scores of black students on the Scholastic Aptitude Test (SAT), which increased 54 points from 1976-1994; white student scores showed no significant change during the same period.

Part of this is what supplies and equipment a school district can afford. With fewer financial resources, students are more likely to use older, lower-quality textbooks and have less access to lab equipment and technology. A study analyzing school district funding in major metro areas found that urban schools in predominantly minority communities spent half as much per student as their suburban counterparts. As a result, the senior high school in East St. Louis (where 97%

of the residents are black) lacks lab tables and dissecting kits in its biology department, while schools in the surrounding suburbs have full chemistry and biology labs to rival those used by professionals in the field. This disparity in technology extends beyond the school building. Minority families who rent their homes are particularly less likely to have consistent access to the internet and connected devices they can use for education, at a rate 3 times as high as white renters. This limits access to online schooling or other resources that could help make up for lack of funding within school districts.

Even more critical than books and devices are the teachers and curriculum a school offers. The data shows that students learn more and perform better on tests when they are able to form a personal relationship with their teachers and fellow students. To do this, the classes need to be relatively small, especially at the elementary school level. Non-special education class sizes in majority-minority schools are 80% larger on average than those in majority-white schools, meaning teachers have less time to devote to each student and are less likely to form those personal connections.

The quality of the teacher's education matters, too. An analysis of 900 school districts in Texas by Harvard economist Ronald Ferguson found teacher expertise the single most influential factor in student educational success, accounting for roughly 40% of the measured variance in math and reading achievement in K-12 students. These findings are supported by a study of 300 first-graders conducted by University of Chicago professor Robert Dreeben. When students received comparable instruction, there was no measurable difference between the reading skill level of students based on race, but many of the black students in his study received sub-par instruction, resulting in an overall achievement gap between black and white students by the end of their first grade year.

In Ferguson's analysis of Texas districts, students in the schools with the highest minority enrollments had a less than 50% chance of having a math or science teacher with a license and degree in their field.

Having fewer and less-qualified teachers also limits how many and what type of courses a school can offer. It takes an expert educator to create a challenging, high-quality curriculum that pushes students to achieve. An analysis of data from the National Educational Longitudinal Surveys and High School and Beyond Surveys, shows that student course-taking record is the best indicator of their test scores. When analyzed this way, the differences between ethnicities were negligible. Further, there's heavy data to indicate students will rise to the expectations placed on them. One experiment randomly assigned 7th-graders who'd been classified "at risk" to remedial, typical, and honors math classes. Those placed in the honors class consistently outperformed the other two groups, rising to the challenge of the pre-algebra curriculum.

Inequality in education funding means wealthier families can provide their kids with better education that gives them more opportunities to create their own wealth as adults. Because their districts can't pay as much or hire as many people, minority students are twice as likely to be taught by ineffective teachers, more likely to be in large classes, and less likely to graduate high school or attend college than their white counterparts.

Early Guidance and Role Models

School is the easiest place for kids to find role models and mentors outside the home. Many people can still name their favorite elementary and high school teachers decades later because of the pivotal impact they had on the individual's life path. Aside from classroom teachers, schools employ athletic coaches, music teachers, and support staff like nurses and counselors who can take on a similar mentorship role.

Support staff, arts programs, and extra-curricular activities are at most risk to be cut when an under-funded district is struggling to meet their budget (if they were even offered in the first place). This still leaves classroom teachers as potential mentors, but if they're poorly-trained and overwhelmed with large classes, they won't be able to offer much personal attention. This puts the onus on families to fill in those gaps and provide the support and guidance kids need, but a lack of generational wealth makes it far less likely an adult in the family can afford not to work. It compounds the issue that black children are the most likely to grow up in single-parent households. Black Americans make up about 12.4% of the total U.S. population, but about 30% of solo parents and 83% of families with a single head-of-household; 84.4% of black mothers serve as the sole, primary, or co-breadwinner for their families, compared to around 60% of white and Latina mothers. It's not unrelated that black men are incarcerated at higher rates than men of other races, accounting for 34% of the male prison population.

There are other ways for kids to get guidance and role models. For instance, extended family, religious groups, and other members of the community can serve this function, too. But the fact remains that most students in under-funded districts have more limited options than those in well-supported districts, and the majority of students in those under-funded districts are racial minorities.

College and Young Adulthood

Over the course of their career, the median bachelor's degree holder earns $1.28 million, more than twice as much as the $630,000 earned in the median career of someone with only a high school-level education. A college education is a wealth-builder in the long term. Wealth enables families to save for college so students don't have to rely on scholarships or take out massive loans. This isn't just helpful for paying for college, but it can also mean students don't need to work to support their day-to-day life. This allows them to focus on their classes and leaves more time to participate in groups and clubs, forming social and professional connections that make it easier to start their career.

Kids who attend well-funded school districts are better-prepared for college academically, and more likely to have the high test scores, competitive course loads, and extra-curricular activities that the top schools look for in applicants. The quality of a student's high school education is reflected in more than just their SAT scores. Schools with lower funding are less likely to offer AP classes that let high schoolers earn college credit and test out of general education classes, so their graduates enter college already a step behind some of their peers.

That's really what it comes down to in the end: generational wealth provides a shortcut for the next generation. A familial safety net also makes it easier for people to take risks, whether that's studying their passion or starting a business. It means parents can afford to loan their kid money for the down-payment on a home in a nice neighborhood, where their property will increase in value and their own kids will receive a high-quality education. All of these things are still possible without wealth, but in most cases it'll take longer to get there and the cost of failure is much higher.

WHAT'S IN A NAME?

We've talked about name bias a bit already in chapter 2. For anyone who forgets, name bias is discriminating against or forming assumptions about an individual based solely on their name, over the other qualities they possess. An example would be assuming José Rodriguez doesn't speak fluent English even though he has a degree from an American university, or hiring Li Chen instead of Destiny Evans for an accounting position, despite the fact that Li is inexperienced and Destiny's been a CPA for 10 years.

A field study conducted in 2003 tested the impact of name bias on the hiring process—and the findings were alarming. The study co-ordinators sent fake resumes in response to more than 1,300 classified ads posted in Chicago and Boston newspapers. Each resume for a given industry was identical except for the names. The resumes that had been assigned white-sounding names, like Greg Baker and Emily Walsh, received a call back for roughly every 10 resumes sent. Those with black-sounding names, like Jamal Jones and Lakisha Washington, had to send 15 resumes before receiving a call back.

These trends held true when the study runners swapped the resumes they sent for one with higher-level qualifications. The superior resume with a white name attached earned about 30% more call backs than the basic one. With a black-sounding name, there was no significant change; the high-quality resume still saw about a 1:15 call back to send ratio. While the call back rates varied by industry, the degree of separation between white- and black-sounding names remained consistent in all the occupations they applied to.

There are ways for companies to reduce this kind of name-based discrimination (which we'll talk about in more detail in part III), but that doesn't change the fact that these statistic reveal: consciously or not, hiring managers are more likely to call a white applicant in for an interview than a black applicant, even when their qualifications are identical. It's a double-whammy when you consider the factors brought up earlier in the chapter. People of color already often face more obstacles to getting the same education and experience as their white cohorts, but even overcoming those odds doesn't completely put them on a level playing field.

RACE AND CAREER PROGRESS

Officially, segregation in the United States ended in the 1960s, but just because it stopped being legally sanctioned didn't make the practice disappear. In practice, America today is still a very segregated nation, and while this is more severe in some areas than others, the majority of white Americans grow up in communities of people who mostly look like they do. When they get to a more diverse college campus or workplace, they seek out the people they think they can relate to and, based on their life experience, that ends up being other white people. It's not an active choice to avoid people of other races, in most cases, but the result is the same whatever the motivation: their professional network ends up being predominantly, if not exclusively, white.

It's an open secret in the job search world that many positions never make it to job boards. Many of these jobs are instead filled through referrals. As late as the early '90s, about 86% of available jobs didn't appear in classifieds and about 80% of executives were hired through networking. The advent of the internet opened the market significantly, but even so about a third of jobs today are filled through referrals, and roughly 42% of businesses offer referral bonuses to current team members.

This is a problem if you're a mostly-white company looking to improve your diversity. A recent study showed that minority women especially are left out by referral systems, and are about 35% less likely to receive a job referral than white men. The jobs that hire through referrals tend to be more white-collar and high-level positions over entry-level or blue-collar work. Without this professional network to draw on, it's harder to start a career as a black American. Black women especially are more likely to work in low-wage industries that don't offer health insurance and other benefits, and have long working hours that limit their time to seek or prepare for better opportunities.

Across industries, pay rates are also lower for black Americans than white Americans. Again, this impacts black women the most. An analysis in 2012 found that black women on average earn $0.64 for every $1 made by the average white man. This disparity remained even for those who obtained advanced degrees. A white man with just a Bachelor's earns, on average, $7 more per hour than a black woman with a Master's degree or higher. Over their career, the average black woman would need to work until age 84 to earn what a white man will by age 60. Alumni surveys from Harvard Business School and Harvard Law School show even a prestigious degree doesn't protect from this completely, and black graduates reported lower career satisfaction and progress over a decade post-graduation.

Part of this disparity is because there are more obstacles to advancement for employees of color. The same familiarity bias that limits job referrals also affects who receives professional development and mentorship within the workplace, especially the informal mentorship that happens on a day-to-day basis in professional settings. Black professionals also feel more limited in their ability to express themselves and share their perspective when they're working in a mostly-white work environment. A survey of professionals with a Bachelor's degree or higher showed black employees reported the lowest levels of coworker and manager support and more consistently said they didn't feel like they fit in their workplace. Research conducted by Georgetown University in conjunction with Gallup showed similarly lower engagement, commitment, and feelings of support among black employees, especially those at the management level, who were consistently more likely to leave their organization than white leaders. As Laura Morgan Roberts of *Harvard Business Review* concludes, "It's clear that the norms and cultural defaults of leadership in most organizations create an inhospitable environment that leaves even those black employees who have advanced feeling like outsiders—and in some cases pushes them out the door."

There is also what Roberts describes as an "emotional tax" of being black in the workplace. When there's limited diversity, the representatives of minority groups are put in a position of being cultural ambassadors, forced to serve as spokespeople for their entire culture along with performing the job they're paid to do. A heightened sense of being different can lead to feelings of isolation and make it more difficult to contribute and share opinions in the workplace. Others feel a need to conform to the workplace standards, altering their hair, dress, speech, and mannerisms to match white coworkers, which can lead to authenticity tension and feelings of shame and resentment over hiding their true self. Experiencing racism in the workplace takes an emotional toll, as well, whether that racism is overt or takes the form of microaggressions and aversive racism, where white employees avoid minority coworkers or change their behavior when they're around.

These extra challenges and pressures mean that people of color often have to be more strategic in managing their careers than white professionals. Aggregated data from Gallup shows professionals of color experienced more job changes and career plateaus than white professionals. This is backed by a 6-year study conducted by professors from Harvard Business School, who found people of color were forced to prove their competency more than white peers to achieve the same promotions, and often had to wait longer between opportunities.

RACE AND LEADERSHIP

About 12% of the current U.S. workforce is black, roughly in line with the overall representation in the population. This percentage drops steeply once you get above the entry level. Black Americans hold only about 8% of the managerial positions, and 3.8% of CEO positions. At the Fortune 500 level, people of color hold only 16% of board seats, with only 3 black CEOs between them (down from a high of 12 in 2002). Some sectors are particularly unfriendly to black leaders, like finance (2.4% of executives), tech (1.9% of executives), and law (1.8% partnership rate from 2005-2016).

The black leaders who do manage to secure these executive positions often find themselves at a disadvantage once they achieve them. A study conducted by professors at Cornell and Emory Universities showed black leaders were disproportionately given tasks they called "glass cliff" assignments, which had a high risk of failure, while other data shows they're more often put in charge during times of crisis and upheaval, where their odds of success are lower. Even in calmer times, black leaders often struggle with similar constraints on their personality and work approach as workers of color in general. They feel pressured, not just to conform, but to downplay their passion and authority out of a concern these will be seen as aggression. This impulse can impede their ability to take charge and assert their leadership abilities when the need arises, putting them in a catch-22 situation when it comes to establishing credibility as a leader. Implicit biases from stakeholders or other executives can mean they doubt the leader's competence from the start. Any mistake or failure is interpreted as a confirmation of their suspicions, making them more likely to blame and remove the leader when something goes wrong—and fear of that scenario adds an additional pressure to leaders of color, above those felt by white leaders.

With all of these obstacles, it's clear why surveyed Harvard Business School graduates of color expressed lower interest in being executives at Fortune 500 companies than white graduates. The steep path to leadership becomes a deterrent, further limiting the number of candidates available to increase executive diversity and perpetuating the cycle.

THE BOTTOM LINE: YES, RACE MATTERS

Race is a core aspect of an individual's identity that influences the culture they were raised into and how they interact with the world. From that point of view race will always—and should always—matter in the sense of being something that's acknowledged and respected. This isn't to say that all people of the same race share a singular experience. It's more that this is one thread of the greater tapestry, one that's impossible to untangle from other developmental factors like economic status, family structure, and community.

Unfortunately, race also still matters when it comes to what opportunities and choices an individual will have in their life. The data is clear: a white child and black child raised in the same neighborhood, with similar economic and family situations, will often have different experiences and opportunities because of their race. The sustained effort put into creating a more equal society has lessened this opportunity gap, and the disparity is less than it was 50 years ago, but this work is by no means finished. To say we are living in a post-racial world is, at best, naively optimistic.

CHAPTER 5:

How Does Bias Affect the Workplace?

Researchers have attempted to quantify the financial cost of bias for American companies. Findings published by Impact Group estimated it as $64 billion a year based on the cost to replace workers who leave their jobs because of discrimination or bias. That figure doesn't account for productivity loss among employees who stay and suffer through a biased workplace. A study from the Center for Talent and Innovation found employees who perceive bias are 3 times as likely to be actively disengaged, behavior that costs US companies somewhere between $450 and $550 billion a year. And each of these studies only looks at one consequence of bias; they don't account for other, harder to track impacts, like the cost of unrealized potential when individuals are unfairly overlooked for promotions—or, on the other side, the cost of mistakes made by the less-qualified colleagues promoted in their place.

Bias impacts every aspect of an organization, from who's made part of the team to how major decisions are made. It has an equally profound impact on the individuals who are on the losing end of it. In a biased team, those from under-represented groups feel the need to be constantly on guard against discrimination, while at the same time carrying the additional burden of being asked to represent their entire community. They often feel the need to alter their behavior to conform with the majority—to "talk white" or "act straight", or repress their emotions so as to avoid being seen as a stereotype, and this false persona can be exhausting to maintain and lead to internal struggles over authenticity and identity. Other times they're ostracized from cliques, then accused of being anti-social or not engaging with their colleagues. "Death by a billion paper cuts" is how one respondent described it in a 2020 *Fortune* article on being black in corporate America.

Identifying the impacts of bias on your organization is an important first step to addressing the problem. Let's look at some of the most ways bias impacts the workplace so you can be better prepared to spot them in your team.

BIAS REINFORCES A HOMOGENOUS ENVIRONMENT

Hypothetical company ABC Inc. has an entirely white, male workforce and leadership. They realize this is a problem, and actively search for and hire a black woman to fill their next opening—only to have her take a job with a competing company 6 months later. This happens a few more times: they hire to increase diversity and the person quits within a few months, or ends up being a low-level contributor who doesn't engage or get along with the rest of the team. After a few years of this effort with little to show for it, the frustrated CEO of ABC Inc. decides there just aren't enough qualified candidates and abandons their diversity initiatives. But he's drawn the wrong conclusion from the data. The candidates weren't the problem; the company's efforts at diversity were doomed to failure from the beginning.

As humans, we find comfort in the familiar. Like pattern recognition, this started as a survival instinct: things that were different or unknown could be dangerous. The flip side of this is that being in an unfamiliar situation makes most people uncomfortable. There's a similar evolutionary impulse behind our tendency to form groups with similar people, which is another type of bias—affinity bias, or a preference for things or people you relate to. When these come into play in a homogenous group, they create an environment that's unfriendly to anyone who doesn't belong to the majority. Being excluded from conversations and social outings limits a non-conforming employee's chances to find mentors and form connections that could further their career; being talked over and ignored in meetings or collaboration sessions leads the employee to the conclusion it's pointless to speak up. When every interaction tells someone they don't belong, their natural reaction is to leave.

Even if under-represented groups aren't intentionally excluded, it's not comfortable to be the proverbial square peg in a sea of round holes. A homogenous group is likely to share values, traditions, and cultural touchstones that may not be universal to other communities. This makes it harder to form social bonds since there are likely fewer shared experiences to build off of. It also means fewer allies to open up to when the individual experiences workplace biases. Colleagues who have never faced discrimination, or never been the target of a microaggression, can't relate to the emotional toll the same way as someone who's had the same experience. They may empathize but can't completely understand, and are more likely to dismiss it as harmless or tell the victim they're over-reacting.

In a bias-free world, it would be entirely possible and logical to make a workplace more diverse a little bit at a time, gradually hiring a variety of perspectives over time. Unfortunately, this more often leads to the situation experienced by our hypothetical company above. A mostly-homogenous workplace allows biases to take root in the culture and processes; as a result, those who don't conform are prevented from making meaningful contributions and, eventually, chased out of the organization.

Is a homogenous workplace bad?

We talked a few chapters ago about the benefits that come from having a diverse team, but is there anything actually wrong with having a homogenous workplace? Members of homogenous teams are more comfortable and experience less conflict, so there are perks to everyone sharing a worldview. As a consequence, though, homogenous teams are less rigorous in their decision making, and while they can arrive at a solution more quickly it's because they don't explore as many options first, so the solution they find is less likely to be the best one possible.

MIT Professor Evan Apfelbaum came to these conclusions in a study he conducted using groups formed from a real-life jury pool. Juries were formed to be either racially diverse or all-white, then given the same case to deliberate. The diverse juries spent more time deliberating the case and considered more angles before reaching their conclusion. Their discussion was also more precise, with fewer factual inaccuracies. These added perspectives weren't just contributed by the non-white jurors. The white jurors on the diverse juries contributed a broader range of ideas and were more accurate in their statements than those in all-white groups. Simply being in a diverse group seemed to change how they thought.

This doesn't just happen with all-white groups, either. In an interview with Martha E Mangeldorf in *MIT Sloan Management Review Magazine*, Professor Apfelbaum cited a study conducted in both North America and Asia that used a similar format to his jury study. This time, groups were given real money and competed in groups to make the best trades on a market simulation. Even in a competitive environment, the homogenous groups made more mispricing errors, tending to over-value trades. They were also more likely to copy the moves made by their competitors, even if the choice was a mistake; participants seemed to assume the other members simply knew something they didn't. This led to pricing bubbles forming in the homogenous groups at a much higher frequency. In the racially diverse groups, participants were more skeptical of the moves made by their competitors, and more likely to make a move that went against the majority.

This happens specifically because diverse teams are uncomfortable. Being in a diverse group keeps the brain from resorting to its default settings, and this makes people more objective and able to make higher-level connections they might not have noticed if their brain wasn't in high gear. The lack of a clear, visible majority also encourages members to think more independently and share differing opinions more freely than they would in a homogenous group. This cuts down on potential blind spots in two ways: there are more diverse perspectives considering the problem from more angles, and each of those perspectives takes a broader view.

One last case study to consider from Professor Apfelbaum's research. Groups in this one were given clues from a murder case and asked to decide which suspect to arrest. In keeping with other studies, the more diverse team identified the right suspect more often—but the homogenous teams were more confident in their choice, even when they'd identified the wrong person. These findings suggest homogenous teams are more likely to fall victim to over-confidence that can blind them to issues with their decision making. This should also serve as a caution to decision-makers. Confidence is easy to mis-interpret as correctness, but it could just as easily come from not having considered all of the options.

BIAS CAN BE CODED INTO AI

In 1988, a medical school in the UK was found guilty of discrimination by the Commission on Racial Equality. The computer program they were using to pre-screen applicants was found to be biased against women and those whose names sounded non-European. The program itself was working well; it matched the decisions made by human admissions staff with a 95% accuracy rate. Because it had been trained using biased data, it made biased decisions—and, in the process, shone a spotlight on the school's deeper issues.

Similar examples abound. Amazon had to scrap their automated recruiting program after it was shown to favor applicants that used masculine or male-coded language. The algorithm used by Broward County, Florida's criminal justice department to label high-risk defendants was found to mis-label black defendants at twice the rate of white defendants in a report by ProPublica.

This doesn't mean that technology is racist. Used correctly, AI can be a powerful tool against bias because it can be trained to ignore factors like race and gender. When biases pop up in algorithms, they come from the humans who designed them and the data sets used to train them. AI systems make decisions in a similar way to the human brain: they look for patterns in an established dataset that can guide them to the correct decision when presented with unfamiliar data in the future. If it's trained to make decisions based on a biased dataset, it will make the kind of biased decisions that landed the British medical school in hot water. Similar problems can occur if it's fed an incomplete dataset. An algorithm trained to pick out the best applications from an all-white data set may rule out other races as not fitting within the standards, even if this wasn't explicitly coded into it. Nobody intended to create a racist algorithm; this was the unfortunate consequence of using a narrow training dataset.

At the moment, about 20% of HR departments use AI in some form, a number that's growing at an accelerating rate. The more sophisticated these programs become, the more difficult it becomes to identify the source of coded biases and remove them from the algorithms. Of course, the best option is to avoid coding them into the system in the first place. A diverse team of programmers, using diverse training data, will be the most likely to code an inclusive AI system. Even with these optimal conditions, it's smart to test the algorithm periodically with fairness programs, such as a counterfactual fairness test, which swaps sensitive attributes on otherwise identical data to ensure the model is making unbiased decisions.

In many ways, removing bias from AI systems is easier than removing them from a person's decision-making process. An algorithm won't get offended when you call out its biases, for one thing. The process is also more transparent with a software program; even with complex code, a sharp eye can pinpoint the source of bias. It's up to the humans using the program to notice and remove this bias, though, and existing structural and personal biases can stand in the way of correcting these problems.

WHY IS BIAS AN ENGAGEMENT KILLER?

In 2017, *Harvard Business Review* surveyed more than 3,500 full-time professionals with at least a Bachelor's-level education, and asked them to assess themselves on 6 workplace traits: ability, ambition, commitment, connections, emotional IQ, and executive presence. They were then asked to assess how their superiors felt about them. A difference between how they rated themselves and how they thought a superior would rate them was analyzed as indicating perceived bias in that category from their supervisor.

Roughly 9.2% of the respondents reported perceived bias in at least two categories. Comparing this group's answers on survey questions to those who didn't perceive bias, they were 4 times more likely to report feeling alienated at work and about twice as likely to feel angry or cynical about their work. These employees were also 60% more likely to have looked for other work in the past 6 months, and 20% of them said they felt disengaged; in contrast, only 7% of those who didn't perceive bias reported feeling disengaged with their work.

When you perceive biases against you, it can be very demotivating. Workers of color often feel held to a stricter standard than white coworkers. They have to prove themselves more to win promotions while watching less qualified colleagues rise through the ranks; they're penalized for mistakes white colleagues are given a pass for. After a while, it can start to feel pointless to even put in the effort, and the employee becomes disengaged.

The targets of bias aren't the only ones affected by it, either. Those who observe bias happening around them in the workplace come to see it as an unfair environment, where people are rewarded because of who they are rather than what they do. Conflicts can result between coworkers, or between team members and management, over how promotion and pay decisions are made, creating a hostile or toxic environment for everyone—and this has a number of other consequences, like:

Ideas aren't shared as freely

In her book *The Fearless Organization*, Amy C. Edmondson explains the importance of creating a psychologically safe atmosphere for employees. An environment of "open candor", as she describes it, allows everyone to share their ideas and concerns without fear of punishment or embarrassment. Those who work in this kind of environment are more interested in life-long learning, form stronger connections with coworkers, and are more invested in the success of their team and company.

The *Harvard Business Review* study mentioned above supports this data. Among those who perceived bias from superiors, 34% said they regularly withhold ideas or solutions at work. This likely isn't out of any feeling of spite; more likely, they've learned from experience they'll be talked over, ignored, or even ridiculed if they share their ideas.

A psychologically safe environment goes hand-in-hand with inclusivity. Those who work on inclusive teams with a culture of open candor are 87% less likely to perceive bias from supervisors. It also fosters an environment of greater innovation since employees feel safe bringing their best ideas to the table, and can prevent missteps since employees aren't afraid to ask questions and challenge the boss' decisions.

Talents are mis-used

A study of Danish companies published in *American Economic Journal* looked at biases as they relate to ethnicity and who gets promoted in organizations. In the study, instances were identified where a person was promoted who matched the ethnicity of the decision-maker but wasn't the most productive or qualified employee. The study determined these companies had foregone 8% of their potential earnings, on average, due to these biased choices.

It's difficult to perceive the lack of something, and this impact of bias in particular tends to go unnoticed for that reason, but it's just as potentially damaging in terms of talent loss as high turnover. This doesn't only happen when people are up for promotions, either. A manager might fail to choose a black employee for an important project, even though they have the exact skillset the job requires, depriving the employee the opportunity to excel. The team is weaker as a result, too, because a less-qualified person is working in their stead. Everyone loses when talent is mis-used in the workplace.

This starts at the very beginning of an employee's time with the company. Biased decisions about who gets access to mentorship and sponsorship can mean some employees get more investment in their career growth than others based on their gender or race rather than their potential. The ones who get more attention will be more likely to stick around long-term and better prepared for opportunities to rise to the leadership level. This ultimately prevents the leadership team from becoming more diverse and gaining the benefits that could provide.

THE EFFECTS OF BIAS ON EMPLOYEES

Most of this chapter has focused on how bias affects the workplace. Employees are a crucial part of every workplace, too, and the ways bias affects their health and happiness can't be overlooked in any discussion of the topic.

By now, it should be clear how bias stymies career progress. Those who don't fit the mold have limited access to mentorship and growth opportunities that could further develop their talents. If they're not chosen for big assignments they can't gain the accolades that would put them on the path to advancement, while being ostracized from conversations and social circles makes it harder to build a professional network that would open up opportunities. Bias doesn't kick in at the moment a promotion is offered. It's the cumulative effect of being consistently under-valued that leads many to downgrade their career aspirations and prevents workers of color from reaching their full potential.

The National Institute of Health took a different look at the effect of discrimination, evaluating its effect on both mental and physical health. Experiencing discrimination in the workplace showed a strong correlation with increased risk of cardiovascular illness, high blood pressure, and obesity, as well as mental health symptoms like anxiety, depression, traumatic stress, and imposter syndrome. Like victims of sexual harassment, those who face bias are also more likely to engage in harmful behaviors like alcohol abuse and smoking, which are used as a coping mechanism.

A business runs best when workers are healthy and enabled to do their best work. Bias creates an environment where that's not possible for everyone on your team. That alone should be reason enough to want to eliminate it from your organization.

CHAPTER 6:

Barriers to Inclusion

For a lot of readers, the last five chapters only reinforced what you already knew: diversity is a good thing, and bias does real harm to both organizations and the individuals who belong to them. It's not that you don't want an inclusive culture, it's that you don't know how to create one—and every time you try, it feels like there's something new standing in your way.

Resistance to creating a more inclusive culture can come from the leadership, the individual members, or the structure and policies of the organization itself. Figuring out the source of bias can be a complex process in itself. Let's look at some of the most common barriers to inclusion in organizations, along with some general approaches you can use to overcome them.

STRUCTURALIZED BIAS

Most diversity education focuses on deconstructing individual biases. This is helpful, certainly, but it ignores a major potential source of discrimination and unfairness in the workplace: the biases that have been built into the structure of the organization through stereotyped language, unfair or inequitable policies, and systems that make it easier for certain groups to advance and thrive than others.

Structuralized bias allows discrimination to persist in an organization even if individual members aren't actively perpetuating them (or, in some cases, are actively working to create an inclusive workplace). If your company's efforts to improve diversity and inclusion keep failing and you're not sure why, very often structuralized biases are the root of the problem—and, just like personal biases, they can go unnoticed for a surprisingly long time if no one's consciously working to root them out.

One common example of this kind of structuralized bias is a company grooming policy that forbids Afro-centric hairstyles like braids, dreadlocks, or afros. This reinforces white privilege in the workplace because it links "professional grooming" with European hairstyles. Even aside from the way this limits self-expression, a grooming policy that bans Afro-centric hairstyles forces employees with kinky hair to take extra steps to be considered presentable in the workplace. This puts an additional time and money burden on non-white employees, similar to how expectations that women workers wear make-up puts an additional burden on female employees compared to their male counterparts.

A biased grooming policy is one of the easier structural biases to spot. Others are so pervasive even those from the affected groups may not be able to identify them right away. In an article on Forbes, Janice Gassam Asare cites the example of a female CEO who wanted to create a more equitable workplace, but was having difficulty getting women to apply to openings. Consulting with a diversity expert revealed that she was using male-centric language in her job postings. This wasn't done on purpose; the CEO in question was simply using the common language of her industry. The issue came down to the gender-based cultural norms that this language was based in and perpetuated. Once she identified and changed the problematic wording, she immediately saw a shift in the gender distribution of applicants.

This is often what makes undoing structural biases so difficult. These practices and policies were acceptable when they were written, but they were written under an inequitable system. Deconstructing them often means also tearing down the industry norms that allowed them to perpetuate in the first place, something that's not easy to do from within an organization—especially if the top leadership has never had the lived experience of their identity putting them at a disadvantage.

Improving Biased Policies

The process for undoing structural biases is two-fold. First, individual members of the organization have to do the personal work to be aware of and reduce their own biases. Bias education lays the groundwork for this kind of self-discovery, giving individuals the knowledge and tools to scale this awareness to the institutional level so they can begin to call out problematic policies.

Once your team has the language and awareness to spot systemic bias, the second step is to remove these policies and replace them with a more equitable alternative. That second part is key. You can't just tear down a system without having something to use in its place; this is likely to result in chaos and instability rather than meaningful, lasting change. Be intentional and deliberate in shaping the new policy, down to the words you choose at a sentence level, to make sure you're not just replacing one biased policy with another.

Replacing biased policies and practices is always the best option, but when that's not possible there are other ways to minimize their impact. Consider implementing an appeal process for employees who feel unfairly targeted by biased policies. You can also improve existing policies by making them more flexible rather than rewriting them from scratch. To use the earlier grooming policy example, broadening the definition of "professional appearance" to include Afro-centric hairstyles maintains the intent of the rule but applies it equally to all employees.

INCONSISTENT STANDARDS AND EXPECTATIONS

Imagine you've planned to meet your best friend for dinner. You arrive at the restaurant on time but they never show up, and don't reply when you text them; after waiting for an hour, you leave. The next day they call and apologize, explaining that they'd had a family emergency. Now imagine that same situation, but the person you were supposed to meet was a blind date. Would you be as inclined to believe they had a real emergency, or would you suspect they're making up an excuse? Waiting for the best friend in the restaurant, would you be worried that something had happened to them or would you be angry that they're not there as planned—and would those feelings change for the blind date?

In this example, it's natural to extend more leeway to the person you already like and trust than a complete stranger. Unfortunately, this same thought framework is often applied to broader groups, an effect known as in-group bias or similarity bias. People who share the individual's trait are seen as more familiar and therefore more trustworthy and more deserving of forgiveness or leeway than those of other races, genders, or backgrounds.

Everyone makes mistakes from time to time, and similarity bias affects how those mistakes are perceived, leading to unequal enforcement of the rules. A white employee shows up late but is spared a write-up when he explains his car broke down on the way to work; that same leeway may not be shown to a black or Hispanic employee, resulting in them having more negative marks on their permanent record and putting them at a disadvantage for future raises and promotions. The end result is a higher standard for those who don't fit the majority, limiting their access to leadership positions and often driving them from the organization in search of a less frustrating environment.

Equalizing Praise and Discipline

Increased transparency is often the first step toward making sure the rules and standards in your organization apply equally to everyone. Asking managers to fully explain the reasoning behind promotion, pay, and discipline decisions forces them to slow down and examine their process. This alone can make them aware of assumptions or biases that were clouding their judgment, guiding them toward a fairer, more fact-based decision. Sharing this process with employees builds trust in leadership when team members see decisions were merit-based—and allows them to catch any lingering biases that impacted the decision.

In a truly inclusive environment, performance assessments are based on actions, not the person acting. Using an objective, data-based metric in these decisions can help keep that the focus in your organization.

LACK OF MENTORS AND ROLE MODELS

Most mentorship that goes on in an organization doesn't happen because of a formal mentorship program. It happens more organically when a senior member chooses to give advice and guidance to a younger colleague. In a mostly homogenous workplace, this often leads to minority members being left out of the equation. Senior members are more likely to offer their advice to colleagues they see as similar, for one thing. Trust is key in a mentor/mentee relationship, too. In a psychically unsafe workplace, where those not part of the in-group regularly experience microaggressions or outright racism and sexism, an offer of advice or mentorship can come across as a dismissal of their competence, or an implication that they need help because they're not good enough to be there.

Having a diverse group of senior members helps to equalize informal mentorship, but there's a definite catch-22 there: if diverse team members aren't receiving mentorship, it's less likely they'll stick around long enough to become senior members. A similarly cyclical problem can be seen in professional networks. Because fewer professionals of color are hired by organizations, many white professionals don't have many (if any) non-white network contacts, which leads to them recommending other white colleagues for openings—leading to fewer professionals of color being hired.

Equalizing Mentorship Access

A formal mentorship program is one option, though it's not as simple as pairing people off at random. The basis of a successful mentor/mentee relationship is trust, and building that means establishing connections based on shared values and interests. The mentee will only get the full benefits from the relationship if the mentor is committed, and vice versa.

Senior members in organizations are really the ones in the driver's seat, here. It's up to leaders and experienced team members to pay attention to who they choose to share their knowledge with. If you're in a position to be a mentor, try to connect with everyone on your team, not just those who look like you. If you've never had a full conversation with some of the junior team members, start that dialogue to find out what you have in common. It may take a bit of extra effort to build a relationship, but that effort is necessary if you want to build an inclusive environment.

OUT OF TOUCH LEADERSHIP

Early attempts to build diversity in organizations used a quota system. It's easy to see the logic behind this: if the problem is an overly homogenous workforce, requiring HR to hire more diverse employees will fill in those gaps. The issue with this approach is that it doesn't ask why the staff was so homogenous in the workplace, and whether the environment was a friendly one for people who didn't fit the mold.

The issues with quota-based diversity have been well established by this point, but many leaders still default to this approach. It isn't just because they're stuck in their ways, though this may be part of it. Those who have only experienced leading a homogenous team lack the skillsets required to build an inclusive environment, and often even the insight to see that this is necessary. They may not see diversity and inclusion as primary concerns because they've never been the target of race-based bias. Since they've never experienced a diverse workplace, the potential benefits of increased diversity are intangible, and don't carry weight against the real-world problems that they deal with on a day to day basis. As a result, diversity initiatives are viewed as negotiable, or even expendable when in times of crisis.

Getting Through to Out-of-touch Leaders

In the ideal environment, leaders are the agents of change. When that's not possible, you at least need their full support to make the policy changes and culture shifts that allow a diverse workforce to thrive. When you bring a new diversity initiative to the leadership team, don't assume that they understand why it's necessary. Be prepared to spell it out in detail, and back up what you say with both personal anecdotes from team members and data from external experts. If they don't make the connections on their own, help them understand how a more diverse team could help them solve their other business problems, and why diversity initiatives improve engagement and retention.

CHANGE AVERSION

Leaders aren't the only ones in a workplace who can get stuck in their ways. Human beings are hard-wired to resist change. We trust things that have been around for a while more than things that are new; the new is unfamiliar, and that means it could be dangerous.

Removing biases from the workplace disrupts the status quo. Those who have benefitted from it in the past may be particularly resistant to the new system, while others will respond negatively to any change, even one that will make their job easier or their life better.

Learning to Embrace Change

You can't force someone to be comfortable with change, but you can make that change as painless as possible. This starts by announcing the coming change well in advance and explaining why it's necessary, what the benefits will be, what the new policy will look like, and how it will be implemented. Give employees a way to respond to this announcement with their concerns, questions, and suggestions. Just giving someone a chance to voice their reasons for resistance can often make them feel more comfortable with the process even if nothing functionally changes. And you may find your employees' concerns aren't baseless. Opening the process up to feedback means more eyes to expose potential flaws that could lead to chaos and problems down the line. One reason people resist change is that familiar routines give them a sense of control over their environment, and losing that control can be disorienting and anxiety-inducing. The smoother the transition process, the less these daily routines will be disrupted, and the more quickly resistant team members will settle in to the new status quo.

LACK OF AWARENESS AND SENSITIVITY

As the demographics shift within an organization, its culture and policies will also need to evolve. Workplace traditions and social events are likely based around the shared cultural touchstones of the majority group, and can feel exclusionary for those who don't belong to it. Members who have only worked in homogenous teams may make comments or jokes that are inappropriate without realizing why, and require education and guidance to understand how to interact across cultural borders.

Familiarity bias can also be a factor, here. Leadership feels more connected to the people they've been working with the longest, who were the members of the previously homogenous team. When newer team members bring complaints of discrimination based on their race or gender, it's more likely leadership will downplay those concerns, or take the side of the established employee. Instead of having a conversation or consequences that could expose and break down biases, this kind of response from leadership perpetuates bias by making those who experience it less likely to speak up.

That's the underlying problem with a lack of bias awareness: it allows it to continue on, unchecked and often unseen by those of the in-group. Companies may have trouble hiring and retaining diverse employees and be baffled as to why. They look around and see a friendly, supportive workplace because they've never taken the time to listen to how it feels from other perspectives.

Increasing Awareness of Biases

Discussions about discrimination are uncomfortable for everyone at first. Race particularly is a topic of conversation that we have learned to treat as taboo, especially in the workplace, and this taboo status is part of what keeps biases alive. Talking about biases leads to conversations about how to address them. Once you get through that initial discomfort, you can reach an environment of open candor where everyone feels free to share their voice and experiences.

Unconscious bias training and seminars can be a great way to start the conversation. They give employees the language to talk about race, gender, disability, sexual orientation, and other uncomfortable topics productively and without eliciting a defensive reaction. These programs also increase awareness about the existence of bias for those who haven't experienced it, and can start the process of uncovering and deconstructing personal biases.

Having said that, no diversity workshop is going to transform an organization's culture overnight. Once the team has the tools to identify and talk about bias, the next step is coming up with actionable steps to change it—and then actually committing to those changes.

PART III:
Identifying and Reducing Bias

CHAPTER 7:

Diversity and Inclusion: What's the Difference?

Diversity and inclusion go together like two peas in a pod. The terms have become so interlinked that, in corporate environments, they're reduced to the catch-all D&I. Because of this, most organizational leaders will be able to give an answer if you ask about their diversity, but if you follow that up asking about their level of inclusivity most will be confused. In their mind, the two terms are synonymous. But while there's certainly a strong relationship between diversity and inclusion, there are subtle but important differences between the two concepts. Understanding those differences is a crucial first step in building an organization that fully supports all its members.

Clarifying the language you use to talk about diversity in your organization isn't just a question of semantics. If you treat terms like diversity, inclusion, and equality like they're interchangeable synonyms, your organization lacks the nuanced vocabulary necessary to effectively plan and implement new measures to create an environment that's not just diverse, but also is equally comfortable and offers equal opportunities to team members from a variety of backgrounds. Understanding the difference between these concepts is the first step toward creating a truly inclusive organization.

DEFINING DIVERSITY, INCLUSION, EQUALITY, AND EQUITY

In her book *Inclusion: Diversity, The New Workplace, and the Will to Change*, author and thought leader Jennifer Brown gives a concise explanation of the difference between diversity and inclusion. She describes diversity as the who—who is sitting around the table, being recruited, and getting promotions in your organization. Inclusion, on the other hand, is the how. It describes the culture and behaviors within the organization that promote and maintain diversity.

For a more detailed definition, you can think of diversity as the demographic make-up of your workforce and how many different groups are represented. This doesn't only include race, gender, and sexual orientation, though these are the demographics of concern for most modern organizations. Alliant International University's chief diversity officer Rita Mitjans describes four types of diversity that can be found in most organizations:

1. Internal diversity: This is the demographic variation most think of when they hear the term, describing traits like ethnicity and gender identity that are in-born, unchanging characteristics.

2. External diversity: These are characteristics that are developed over time rather than in-born, like their religious beliefs, interests, and passions. These are often long-held beliefs, and could be crucial aspects of their identity, but do have the potential to change over time.

3. Worldview diversity: Similar to external diversity, this describes how team members see the world. It includes things like the individual's political affiliation and core values.

4. Organizational diversity: These are the logistical elements that distinguish people from each other within the organizational

environment, and can include their job title, department, or specialization.

As you can see from this definition, diversity is something that applies to groups of people. A single individual cannot be "diverse." Labeling candidates and team members as diverse is a coded way of saying they don't belong to the dominant group within the organization, and ultimately becomes another form of "othering" that's problematic in its own way. Saying that a black candidate is diverse implies white is the default, unintentionally upholding the biased standard that created a homogenous workforce in the first place.

Obviously there will be a lot of overlap between the first three types of diversity: a person's in-born traits and life experiences will shape their worldview and beliefs. Most diversity initiatives implemented in organizations focus on increasing internal diversity with the goal of having greater worldview diversity, providing the benefits like increased innovation and fewer blind spots that we've discussed in previous chapters. Unfortunately, many organizations stop there, looking only to check all the boxes on their quota sheet without thinking about what other changes might need to happen when your homogenous organization becomes more heterogeneous.

Another common analogy is to say that diversity is an invitation to the party, but inclusion is being asked to dance. This doesn't quite capture the entire difference, though. Inclusion isn't just being asked to contribute—it means having those contributions valued equally by the organization. It goes a step further than diversity, not just acknowledging the differences that exist in the workplace but planning for how all of those voices will be heard and respected. An inclusive workplace focuses on providing a positive experience to all of the humans who work there, allowing everyone to bring their full selves to work and have an equal chance to advance and thrive. To put it another way, inclusion is how diversity comes to life because it allows for those of all backgrounds and identities within a group to work together within an environment of mutual respect.

Equity and equality are another pair of terms commonly thrown around in discussions of diversity and inclusion, and are similarly treated as synonyms when they, in fact, have subtle but significant differences. Equality happens when everyone is treated identically. Equity, on the other hand, means providing identical outcomes by focusing on the needs of individuals. Similar to the relationship between diversity and inclusion, equity is the means by which true equality can be achieved in an organization that has, in the past, not provided an equal playing field to everyone.

An example might be helpful in clarifying this difference. Consider a hypothetical organization in which the majority of employees believe in Christianity, while believers in other faiths are the minority. Giving everyone Christmas Day off of work is an example of equality; all employees get this same day off, but it doesn't have the same meaning for everyone. Equity, on the other hand, could mean giving all employees an extra paid day off during the winter holiday season and allowing them to choose which day they use it. This gives everyone a day off of equal weight, rather than emphasizing the Christian holiday over those of other faiths. Equity acknowledges that individuals within a diverse workplace are going to have individual needs and require different types of support, achieving true equality of both opportunities and outcomes by making these individualized adjustments.

WHAT DOES AN INCLUSIVE ENVIRONMENT LOOK LIKE?

Clarifying the terms used to talk about inclusion is a great first step, but what does an inclusive culture actually look like in the real world?

While there isn't a one-size-fits-all template that fits every single organization, all-inclusive groups do share certain attributes that can be a helpful guide for creating an environment where everyone feels welcomed and included. Consider how many of the statements below could describe your organization. The areas where your current culture falls short are a great starting point for future improvements.

- <u>Policies and procedures are transparent</u>. Everyone in the organization should have the same understanding of the rules and how decisions that affect members are made. Unspoken rules of behavior that apply to some groups and not others reinforce bias and drive inequality because only those who are in the know are able to thrive.

- <u>Rules and standards are consistent for all members</u>. Double-standards that favor one group over another create inequity in the workplace. This is true even if they're based in seniority, hierarchy, or other non-demographic factors. If the rules are different for some people than others, this creates a culture of inequality that allows other biases to perpetuate unchecked.

- <u>All members feel safe to be their true selves</u>. In a group that's diverse but non-inclusive, those who aren't in the majority group often feel the need to mask their identity and alter how they talk or act. Inclusion means everyone can be their full, authentic selves without fear of discrimination.

- <u>Diversity is consistent across levels</u>. If all members of your organization are being given an equal shot at advancement opportunities, the demographic breakdown of the leadership should be at least similar to that of the entire group. Having a highly diverse entry level and a homogenous leadership team is a red flag that all members aren't being given the same opportunities.

- <u>Cultural differences are celebrated, not sterilized</u>. Often, newly-diverse organizations will respond to complaints of inequality by removing the cultural touchstones of the majority, but this approach just means everyone has to hide who they are and makes everyone feel like they're walking on eggshells. In an inclusive environment, members are encouraged to share their unique perspective with the team—it's additive, not restrictive.

- <u>Earned privilege is valued over unearned privilege</u>. Every organization has criteria for who receives promotions, raises, and other accolades. In an inclusive group, these are based on team member actions and observable behaviors, not opinions or subjective factors that could be influenced by unconscious bias.

- <u>All members can report issues and get conflict resolution guidance</u>. Even in a positive workplace, there will be clashes between members from time to time. Healthy organizations have a system in place to resolve conflicts in a way that's confidential, impartial, and non-confrontational for all members involved.

- <u>The organization embraces change</u>. As an organization's membership shifts over time, it periodically needs to review and update its policies to meet their changing needs. Taking a growth mindset that strives for constant improvement allows the organization to evolve in response and ensure it stays welcoming for everyone involved.

CREATING AN INCLUSIVE CULTURE

Belonging is the main keyword to focus on when you're working to build a more inclusive environment. That's ultimately what it comes down to: who feels like they belong in your organization—and how can you make sure the answer is "everyone"? As we've said before, this isn't a one-and-done evaluation. It's a culture that needs to be maintained with small day-to-day checks and adjustments.

This work shouldn't only fall on the shoulders of those who belong to minority groups. Allies in the majority have an especially important role in the building stages of diversity. They're able to have a lower-stakes conversation about bias and discrimination—it might be uncomfortable, but since they're not the target of the bias they're less likely to face reprisal for speaking up (and unfortunately often, more likely to be believed). Allies can help simply by having the self-awareness to know when they should get out of the way and let an under-appreciated colleague have their time to shine. Actively seeking ways to equalize who's given opportunities can go a long way toward expanding diversity upwards through an organization.

While the actions of individuals can help, though, the ultimate goal is to create an inclusive culture that sticks even after the current members are gone. For that, you need to establish systems, not just rely on the positive actions of team members. This gives allies who are leaders and decision-makers the most power in both building a more diverse team and retaining that diversity by providing all members equal support.

Opening up the conversation is the first step. Those in leadership can conduct an employee survey to gauge how far you have to go. Use that "belonging" keyword as the basis of your questions. Ask questions like whether employees feel their voice is heard, and whether they feel they can be themselves in the workplace. Pair this with group dialogues about what inclusion means for the members of your team and what they see as the main impediments in your current culture. Work together to come up with goals and a metric for gauging your success. This allows your D&I initiatives to be tracked and measured like any other business process, and that keeps it from being forgotten or pushed aside as easily as when it exists only as a concept.

Once you've had the conversation, it's time to act. Establish permanent, open communication channels where team members can raise concerns or report instances of bias without fear of reprisal. Implement mentorship and peer-to-peer buddy systems that encourage more conversation and connections between team members of different generations and backgrounds. Sponsor an employee resource group to provide a safe space to marginalized workers and oversee improvements to the day-to-day workspace. When planning events and celebrations, draw from the full range of cultures represented in your group rather than defaulting to those of the majority. You don't need to do all of this at once, either. Small, incremental improvements that are fully supported and have the whole team's buy-in can add up to huge change in the team member experience over time.

How do you choose which steps to take for your organization? The answer to that is deceptively simple: ask the people you're hoping to help. A 2019 survey by *Harvard Business Review* found that those in majority groups consistently under-estimate the day-to-day challenges faced by those in the minority when crafting diversity initiatives. As a result, while about 97% of the companies they surveyed had diversity initiatives, 75% of the employees surveyed from under-represented groups had experienced no benefits from these programs. This is what happens when leaders implement the policies they think team members need, rather than learning what would actually help remove the impediments their team members face in the real world. *HBR* did identify a set of what they called "hidden gem" interventions for different groups. Female survey takers consistently wanted practical ways to advance their careers regardless of their family status, citing programs like childcare assistance, scheduling flexibility, and improved parental leave policies as the most useful. For non-white professionals, policies that reduced bias in decisions about meeting attendance and team selection were rated the most helpful, followed by formal sponsorship and mentorship programs that could expand their professional networks to include senior colleagues. This gets back to the point of equity as a road to equality. Implementing programs that are tailored to your team's individual needs gives everyone the same access to resources and opportunities.

One thing to keep in mind is that it can take a while to unlearn old habits. Those in the majority group may need colleagues' help to spot their biases and change problematic language or behavior. Cultivate a culture of questioning perceived bias, and educate all team members about unconscious bias and how to respond non-defensively if their words or actions are called out. At the same time, those in under-represented groups may need encouragement to share more of themselves. They've likely spent years building and honing their workplace persona, or downplaying certain aspects of their identity to conform with the majority, and may feel uncomfortable breaking this established character. Leaders can help by increasing transparency and walking their talk on equality to earn the team member's trust.

The necessary foundation for all of these changes is a comprehensive anti-discrimination policy that's followed consistently throughout the organization. Make sure you include a diverse mix of voices in crafting this policy. If it's based on biased or limited worldviews, it will be toothless at best and, at worst, could be used as a tool to justify future discrimination.

GOING BEYOND DIVERSITY

In the *Harvard Business Review* survey cited above, half of the respondents who belong to minority groups reported seeing bias in their day-to-day work environment. About the same number of respondents said they don't believe their companies have the right policies in place to keep bias out of major decisions. Remember, 97% of these companies do have a diversity policy. The leaders recognize that they have a problem and they want to fix it, but they're not taking the right steps to create meaningful change. It's not enough to just release a statement telling the world how much you value diversity. An inclusive culture is the result of sustained effort, directed by the individual and self-reported needs of under-represented groups, and supported fully by the leadership. It requires commitment—and a lot of patience. The good news is, it's something any organization can build if they're willing to invest the time and effort to do it the right way.

CHAPTER 8:

Key Traits of an Inclusive Organization

Inclusivity is a complex concept, one that affects every aspect of an organization, and there's no easy, one-size-fits-all roadmap to follow to achieve it. Part of the issue for those who want to create a more inclusive culture is figuring out where to start. Tearing down biases and replacing discriminatory policies takes time and consistent effort, and that's aside from the work of identifying problematic processes and behavior—not always as obvious a determination as it might seem. It can feel overwhelming when you're taking a holistic, big-picture view, and more so if you feel like you're doing it on your own without full buy-in from your leadership and colleagues.

The good news is, you don't need to fix everything all at once. Small, incremental improvements can result in a larger shift in the long-term, and many can be made from the employee or middle-manager level. We briefly looked at the traits of an inclusive workplace in the last chapter. Now, let's dig a bit deeper into each of these concepts, and what steps can be taken from various levels of an organization to foster it.

DEVELOPING INCLUSIVE LEADERSHIP

The work and energy to build an inclusive culture can come from anywhere in an organization, but those in leadership roles usually have the most power and agency to make meaningful change. This doesn't always have to mean re-writing policies, either. How a leader interacts with their reports plays a large role in whether all individuals feel like they belong. Team members look to leaders for how they should behave. A few small adjustments to a leader's thoughts and actions can send positive shockwaves throughout an organization.

For leaders who want to spur this kind of transformation, self-analysis is an excellent first step. Inclusive leaders are self-aware about the unconscious biases they hold and actively work to limit their influences on the decision making process. This kind of self-awareness is crucial in organizations with a clearly-defined hierarchy where lower-ranking individuals may not feel comfortable giving critical feedback to their bosses. Leaders need to be aware of this power dynamic and understand they can't always rely on organization members to tell them if their behavior is a problem.

If you can't rely on others to point out biases—and they're often invisible to those who hold them—how can leaders identify the flaws in their decision-making process? There are some tools that can help. Implicit Association Tests are one way to get a glimpse into unconsciously-held biases. While these tests do have flaws, they're useful in pinpointing areas of thought you need to examine more closely for signs of bias. It can also help to develop stronger empathy and emotional intelligence. An inclusive organization recognizes that its members each have a unique lived experience, and this requires leaders willing to listen to and understand different perspectives. Do independent research into cultures you're not familiar with to better understand their unique needs and challenges. When you don't understand something, don't dismiss it out of hand; respectfully ask for more clarification from members of that community and truly listen to their answers without pre-judgment.

Outside perspectives from other team members can be very helpful for leaders, you just need to be smart in how you solicit them. One option is to separate the decision from you as a leader by posing the question as hypothetical. For example, rather than asking "Am I making a biased decision?", explain the steps you took to reach that decision and ask something like "Where do you see bias in this thought process?" By asking them to critique the process (rather than their boss) it removes some of the risk and discomfort from the question, making it more likely you'll get an honest answer. Seeking out more diverse input makes leaders more aware of blind spots and discriminatory or offensive behaviors they're unintentionally perpetuating. The more collaboration goes into making decisions, the more voices are amplified and the more chances you have to dispel individual biases.

Something else leaders should understand is that inclusion doesn't only happen at the big-picture policy level. Day-to-day interactions are just as important. What you do—and don't do—on an everyday basis can either support or derail larger diversity initiatives, and it's up to individual leaders to ensure it's the former. Keep track when you offer mentorship or feedback to reports to make sure you're distributing that knowledge and support equally. The same goes for assigning high-level projects. Don't automatically give them to the same set of star performers; instead, distribute that work throughout the team so everyone has a chance to excel and reach their full potential. If you see or hear something offensive, even if you think it was unintentional, don't let it slide. Talk with the team about what was said or done, why it was a problem, and what could have been done differently. When team members see leaders actively calling out bias, they'll feel more comfortable doing so themselves. If you're called out as a leader, don't respond defensively; listen to the criticism, admit your mistakes, and make an earnest effort to change. Discussions about race and discrimination are uncomfortable for everyone at first. As a leader, you have the privilege to start that conversation with less personal risk, and can use that privilege to encourage more open dialogue and demonstrate how to receive criticism in a professional, beneficial way.

This same advice applies to any gatekeeper in an organization. For those who aren't familiar with the term, a gatekeeper is someone who controls access to opportunities. This includes those who choose and confirm new members, like hiring managers, resume reviewers, and search committee members. It also includes those who assign work and make decisions about raises and promotions, like team leaders and middle managers, since they control what doors are open for different members of the organization. Improving policies can only go so far if those who enforce them are doing so in a biased way. All gatekeepers need to be given skills and resources to encourage diversity and inclusion if you want to create a culture centered on these values.

Bias in organizations leads to disparity in the employee experience, one that's welcoming to those who align with the majority but hostile to those who are seen as "others." To erase this disparity, you first need to alter the current workplace norms, often over the objections of those in the majority who have benefitted from the old policies and standards, or simply resist change of any kind and don't see why it's necessary. Leaders can't control how members behave or react but they still have a crucial role in creating an environment that's psychologically safe for everyone. Give team members plenty of advance notice for changes and invite them to share any objections or concerns they have. Be open and transparent about why the change is happening, the ultimate goals of the change, and how it will impact team members' day-to-day life. Don't underestimate the value of leading by example, either. If the organization's leadership embraces change, it encourages team members to follow suit.

ENCOURAGING VARIED PERSPECTIVES

Leaders aren't the only ones who make decisions in an organization. Leader decisions carry more weight and have broader implications, but even entry-level employees make choices everyday about how to enforce policies, complete tasks, and interact with others. This is why it's important for diversity to be equally distributed throughout an organization, giving all members access to diverse perspectives.

Of course, as we've seen, diversity doesn't just happen overnight. This can feel like an impossible situation for organizations whose lack of varied voices is preventing them from building the diverse membership that would fill in those gaps. While building diversity within the organization is the end goal, there are other ways to seek input from varied perspectives while you're still working toward this ideal.

First and foremost, when you have limited diversity in an organization it's important to make sure everyone's voice is heard. Every team has members who are more outgoing and those who are more reticent. If you're not actively working to hear every voice, you'll only get the opinions of the first group. Create an environment where everyone can contribute in meetings and collaboration sessions. This doesn't only need to be the work of the leader. Individual contributors are just as able to identify quieter colleagues and help pull them out of their shell. In fact, this can sometimes yield better results, especially for those who are quiet out of a fear of reprimand.

One thing to keep in mind: when you hear from varied perspectives, it's more likely they'll disagree. Being open to a multitude of voices doesn't mean having a diverse army of "yes men." The goal is for individuals to challenge each other—and the organization as a whole—to be better. Once you start actively seeking these varied voices, it's important to reward those whose opinions are different from the collective and engage with them in constructive debate. It may take time to foster a culture where everyone feels comfortable sharing critical feedback, and learns how to do so in a respectful way. It starts with asking difficult questions that encourage members to give their full insights, and is reinforced by celebrating and rewarding those who challenge the status quo.

The members of an organization aren't the only place to find diverse perspectives, either. Input from clients, customers, or event attendees can be an excellent source of feedback. While they don't have the same inside perspective on the process as team members, they're also more likely to be completely honest since they won't fear reprisal for sharing negative feedback. In other cases, it may be helpful to bring in a third-party consultant who specializes in inclusivity and diversity, who can analyze your processes and identify issues in your process that are impeding your efforts.

EQUALIZING ACCESS TO OPPORTUNITIES

We talked briefly about gatekeepers in the leadership section, and they're a crucial consideration when it comes to the equality of opportunities available in your organization. This starts all the way back in the hiring process with which applicants are told about the job, who is encouraged to apply, and who is advanced forward through the process. Once people are part of the team, it doesn't only come down to who is assigned which work. Differing mentorship or professional development opportunities set some employees up to succeed better than others. If only your white male team members are taking advantage of development and advancement opportunities, everyone on the team should be asking why.

One easy way to limit the impact of gatekeeper bias is to not give them access to that demographic information. Removing names and other personal information from resumes helps ensure they're being compared on their accomplishments, not their identity. This kind of blinding is more difficult for promotion or advancement decisions, but you can help keep the conversation based in fact over opinion by using measurable metrics and data to rank the candidates. Of course, the best solution is training gatekeepers to identify and correct their own biases. This starts in their training process and is reinforced by providing educational resources, and having a framework in place that tracks how opportunities are distributed, making inconsistencies easier to spot. It's also important to be aware of wider issues that could be limiting access to opportunities for certain groups. For example, if all of your team building and leadership training happens in the early evening, this excludes many working parents from taking part. A small adjustment can make it more equitable for everyone, whether that's offering on-site childcare, allowing working parents to attend remotely from home, or changing the schedule so these events happen during work hours.

A lot of this work does need to happen at the leadership level, but that doesn't mean individual contributors are powerless to enact change. Established individual contributors can help by offering informal mentorship and guidance to non-majority new hires, helping them build the knowledge and connections that lead to future opportunities. Team building activities can serve a similar function, strengthening the relationships between members from different cultures and backgrounds and in turn fostering more cross-cultural conversation and knowledge sharing.

TRANSPARENT POLICIES AND PROCEDURES

Transparency is often seen as a synonym to honesty, but while these two ideas are related they're not identical. Assuming they are leads to its own problems, and toxic behaviors like backstabbing and bullying can often hide behind a mask of "honesty." Transparency doesn't necessarily mean members share every thought that goes through their head. Rather, it's about creating an open culture where conversation is encouraged and information is shared freely between members at all hierarchy levels. The end goal is encouraging constructive dialogue that welcomes input and feedback, ensuring everyone is working toward the same goals and guided by the same values.

Resistance to transparency is often ego-driven. It can make leaders feel vulnerable to admit mistakes and open their decision making process up to criticism. Other leaders may feel uncomfortable relaxing their control over the workplace by allowing outside input into the process. Transparency often has to start from the top with leaders who set the example, eliminating the stigma of being straightforward in the workplace and giving real answers to questions posed by reports. Ultimately, though, it affects everyone in an organization and maintaining a culture of transparency requires collective effort. Even if you don't have full buy-in from leaders, individual contributors can lay the groundwork for this type of environment.

Transparency means different things for different teams, and there are small steps you can take to start building this idea into your organization from any level. Individual team members can set up a peer-to-peer feedback system for reviewing each other's work and processes, and can help ensure new members fully understand the company's policies, goals, and expectations (rather than letting them make mistakes so they have to learn the hard way). Middle managers can serve as a conduit for ideas between team members and upper leadership, ensuring those who write and enforce policies are hearing and acknowledging feedback from lower levels. They can also help by being consistent in their messaging and behavior, sharing the same information with reports that they do with bosses, taking accountability for their mistakes, and giving credit to reports for accomplishments where it's due. Upper leaders can share company-wide performance and changes with the entire team, whether that information is positive or negative, along with ensuring all organization rules and policies are readily available and clearly understood by all members.

A culture that promotes the open sharing of ideas allows individuals to lead the charge for greater inclusivity, rather than relying on leadership to do all the heavy lifting. Your organization's communication systems are an important part of this, allowing upper-level management to review feedback from lower levels without slowing down the decision process to the point it dulls the company's competitive edge. Giving more agency to mid-level managers can help with this since they're closer to the employee perspective and can be trained to curate the feedback from their teams, resolving the issues that are in their control and passing along higher-level concerns to upper leadership. Employee resource groups can be a useful piece of this puzzle, giving members another avenue for sharing their ideas and getting support. The leadership response to feedback is important, too. Employees won't want to share dissenting opinions if they're stifled, shunned, or punished for doing so.

Along with welcoming feedback from team members, leaders need to be active in providing feedback. The annual performance review shouldn't be an employee's only chance to have a one-on-one conversation with their manager about their performance. In fact, separating performance conversations from raises and promotions is a smart move for greater transparency. An employee is more likely to get defensive about a criticism if their livelihood is at stake. Having more frequent, lower-stakes performance conversations increases trust and honesty, enabling the two-way information sharing that is necessary for an inclusive environment.

This same transparent approach should be taken to any information that affects members of a group. For employees, this means equal and easy access to benefits, discounts, and other perks that come along with their position. Use technology to your advantage by creating an online portal or other self-service option for team members to access these resources. The same goes for conflict resolution and reporting systems in your workplace. The easier it is for members to address issues with colleagues in a way that's respectful and confidential for both parties, the more likely these situations will resolve in a positive, productive way.

ENFORCING POLICIES CONSISTENTLY

In a healthy organization, no member should be surprised when they're disciplined. The rules, expectations, and standards are clearly stated, and members know their role and responsibilities. Just as important, they know the consequences for poor performance or unacceptable behavior, and don't expect to be exempt from these consequences because of their seniority or past accomplishments. Members also know where they stand with supervisors thanks to regular conversations about their performance, and trust managers will work with them to set goals for improvement when they fall short.

Double standards and unspoken rules of behavior are an engagement killer in any organization, and particularly damaging for those striving for inclusivity. One reason they're so insidious is that they often arise out of positive biases. Managers might give their "star performer" a pass on minor infractions based on the logic their strong work earns them greater leeway, or be more hesitant to call out a senior team member for committing microaggressions on the assumption they didn't mean to offend. Whatever the reason, though, hidden or unequal standards allow biases to perpetuate and create inequalities in the member experience.

Transparency is a part of this, too. It's fine if a manager believes consistently strong performance should earn a few free tardies; most of their team members would probably agree. The issue comes up when it's not clear exactly what constitutes "strong performance." The fix isn't always eliminating the practice but instead to make it knowledge all members have access to. In this example, one solution could be a point-based attendance system, effectively making it your organization's official policy that someone who's usually reliable won't be punished if they have a bad week.

While leaders dictate how policies are enforced, the first step in consistent enforcement is identifying places where they're not being imposed equally, and that work can be done from anywhere in an organization. When you see rules applied unfairly as a member, speak up—especially if you're benefitting from those inconsistencies. Accusations of unfairness from someone passed over for promotion may be dismissed as sour grapes, but that's less likely if the one who received the promotion backs up their assertions.

LIVING YOUR CORE VALUES

You've probably picked up on some common themes from the sections in this chapter: open, transparent communication; equality of input and opportunities; consistency in policies, discipline, and rewards. Most organizational leaders would agree all of these things are important if asked, and many probably include them in their mission statement or core values. Unfortunately, there's often a breakdown between these stated values and the actions of individuals. Often this happens because these values aren't clearly communicated and haven't been integrated into the policies and procedures. The leaders are saying the right words, but they're not being acted upon.

Making inclusivity part of your core values is an excellent first step, but one that's practically useless on its own. A company that talks up diversity while perpetuating bias in its day-to-day operations is only virtue-signaling. They want people to think they care about inclusion but aren't fully committed to making it a reality, and this kind of performative approach to diversity only leads to bitterness and distrust from members who see their leadership saying one thing and doing another.

Equality and diversity shouldn't just be buzzwords in your employee handbook. Inclusion happens through the interactions of members, managers, and leaders, and it needs support from all of these areas to succeed. This is an ongoing process that takes a lot of work and an intimate understanding of the organization's interpersonal dynamics. While it's often not possible to correct every problem at the same time, small changes can be self-perpetuating. Increasing transparency around workplace policies can reveal hidden biases; encouraging more open conversation between members can lead them to discover fairer, more efficient ways to distribute their tasks and workload. If it's overwhelming trying to think of how to transform your organization's culture, start smaller and identify one problem area within your power to improve, then build off of this success over time.

At the root of all of these improvements is a learning culture that understands change is inevitable in any healthy organization. Practices and policies should be reviewed regularly to make sure they still fit the needs of the current members. When they don't, members should be empowered to proactively seek change, rather than waiting until someone with authority decides it's a priority. The fruit of this effort will be a more committed, engaged, and productive team of respected individuals eager to contribute their unique talents to the organization's shared goals.

CHAPTER 9:

Identifying and Eliminating Bias

When decisions are made based on stereotypes and assumptions it can have serious negative consequences, regardless of whether any harm was intended—and even when those perpetuating the bias don't realize there's a problem. Having a more diverse team can help mitigate the effects of bias, but that alone can't be relied on to create an inclusive environment. Actively seeking out and tearing down biases isn't easy, but it's work that needs to happen in any organization that's truly committed to diversity and inclusion.

There are three major steps in breaking down an implicit bias. The first step is education about biases and how they form. Step two is questioning and exposing the biases, followed by the final step of unlearning the reflex. How you navigate these steps will change depending on your relationship to the bias you've observed. There are different challenges involved in breaking down your own biases, for example, than when you're trying to "manage up" and improve the behavior of a biased boss. Let's look at some strategies you can use in breaking down your own biases, as well as those in colleagues, managers, and organizations.

PERSONAL BIASES

Understanding that everyone has biases is a good first step to identifying them in your own thought processes. The more types of bias you're aware of, the better you'll be able to see them at play when you make decisions and interact with people on a day-to-day basis. It's also important to get an outside perspective that can help you identify your blind spots. Let your colleagues know that you're working to undo your biases and ask them to help you by calling out things you say or do that may have been bias-driven. When you are called out, either by invitation or spontaneously, thank the person for sharing their honest opinion and reflect on what you said or did from the other person's perspective. Implicit Association Tests (IAT) can also be a helpful tool for identifying potential biases. While these tests aren't perfect, they can help you target the kinds of snap judgments and assumptions you make without realizing it.

The more perspectives you're exposed to, the less likely you'll be to rely on stereotypes and assumptions. Make an effort to expand your sphere of influence to include more individuals whose background and identity differ from your own. For some, this could be as easy as starting a conversation with your black coworkers to find shared points of interest where you can connect. Consuming media can also help you see things from other people's point of view, especially if you live and work in a mostly homogenous environment and don't have many organic opportunities to interact with people from different backgrounds. Read or watch books, shows, films, and other media made by own-voices creators from communities whose perspective you're missing. Follow influential voices from those communities on social media and follow links they post to news stories or opinion pieces, especially when they raise a topic you're unaware of or had a differing view on. The internet is often decried for making it easy to form echo chambers, but it can be just as useful in breaking down these barriers between communities if you use it the right way.

Once you've opened your mind to a variety of perspectives, you need to give those new ideas a chance to influence your decision making. That means slowing your thought process down and analyzing the steps you take to reach a conclusion. Practicing mindfulness can help train your mind to take this slower, more methodical approach. For one thing, mindfulness practices like meditation and yoga reduce stress and anxiety, which can trigger the fight-or-flight response that pushes your brain to take more cognitive shortcuts. You're more likely to fall back on biases when you're thinking under pressure, so form habits that reduce that pressure to have more success uncovering and tearing down your unconscious biases. High stress is also associated with a stronger negativity bias, which is the tendency to react to and remember negative events more strongly than positive ones. Negativity bias makes people less willing to interact with people outside their social group because of past rejection or awkwardness; reducing it allows your mind to be more open to new people and perspectives.

Another positive result of mindfulness is an increase in empathy. By understanding the outside influences on your thought processes, you're more likely to acknowledge that the actions of others may be driven by their environment. This helps you to put interpersonal interactions in their full context rather than pre-judging them based on what you can see in the moment. Along with this, those who practice mindfulness develop a more secure sense of self by increasing their awareness of their thoughts, emotions, experiences, and surroundings. As a result, they're better able to separate their own words and actions from their ego, making them more receptive to criticism and more open to outside feedback that can uncover unconscious biases.

You don't need to join an ashram to practice mindfulness. A 2016 study by professors Adam Lueke and Bryan Gibson found participants who went through a single 10-minute mindfulness training showed less biased behavior and attitudes toward black participants in a trust game afterwards. There are a plethora of guided meditation and mindfulness apps you can download for free if you're not sure where to get started.

BIASES IN PEERS AND REPORTS

The stakes are lower when you call out an equal or subordinate for bias than when you see it in your boss, but that doesn't mean it's a comfortable conversation. Spotting biased behavior from colleagues isn't always a straightforward process, either, especially when they're also your friends. It's human nature to give people you like the benefit of the doubt, and sometimes that can lead to making excuses for their problematic behavior.

Inclusion is a team effort. Getting buy-in from the entire team is the first step to identifying and eliminating biases from its members. This is easier to generate when you're in a management position, but it can also be done from within a team. Step one is clarifying why it's important for team members to uncover their unconscious biases. Explain how biases create disparities in the workplace, and how removing them will help all employees reduce their blind spots and make better, more thoughtful decisions. For leaders convincing budget-conscious colleagues, emphasize how decreasing bias can help you meet both DEI and productivity goals by fostering a most inclusive environment where employees feel valued and contribute their full talents. When the whole team understands the goals of bias reduction, it's easier to set meaningful, achievable goals—and get the support you need to achieve them.

Leading by example is a good way for those in management roles to encourage team members to question biases. Aim for more objectivity in performance reviews, and consider how you assess individuals' performance to make sure you're not generalizing or making assumptions based on their identity. Periodically review your promotion decisions and performance assessments to check for signs of biases you've missed. A good metric is to compare the people you've recommended for promotion or raises against the overall team. They should demonstrate equal levels of diversity. If they don't, you should take a closer look at why.

Along with this self-work, you can encourage your colleagues to speak up about biases—both those they see and their own. Share the biases you've uncovered in your thought processes. Seeing you own your imperfections will make others more comfortable with that level of vulnerability. Organize a training session or provide resources that give team members the vocabulary to call out bias without attacking the individual. When you see offensive or biased behavior, don't let it slide; ignoring it sends the message that the behavior is acceptable. That said, you don't want to push the person into a defensive place. Remember what we said about mindfulness in the section above. Shame, like stress, triggers a fight-or-flight impulse that makes people less open to outside perspectives. In a group setting, asking questions can be a good non-confrontational way push back against biases. If a male coworker describes an outspoken female colleague as "aggressive" in a meeting, probe for more specificity about the exact words or actions that led them to this conclusion. This can help lead peers into questioning their own biases and the assumptions they make.

For deeper conversations, it's often best to take the individual aside and have a private discussion. Waiting to address it also gives you the chance to step back and work through your emotions. It's normal to feel angry if you've been the target of a microaggression, but that anger can shift the focus of the conversation to your reaction rather than the behavior that prompted it. Maintaining a cool head keeps the attention where it should be. Start the conversation by describing the behavior or words that bothered you and why they were offensive or inappropriate. Once you've said your piece, give the other person a chance to respond and explain their perspective. Demonstrating that you respect their voice and individuality can help keep the conversation productive.

BIASES IN LEADERSHIP AND GATEKEEPERS

The leadership level is often the least diverse in an organization, at the same time they're the ones who set diversity goals and have the most influence on policy and decision-making. This can easily derail efforts to improve inclusivity and often feels like an insurmountable obstacle, especially in organizations with poor two-way communication between hierarchy levels. Those working toward a more inclusive environment are put in the difficult situation of potentially risking their employment or status if they call out a leader's bias, or letting it slide and allowing that bias to cause further harm.

Just like with peers and reports, timing and phrasing are key when you're pointing out bias in a gatekeeper or leader in your organization. Your goal should be raising awareness of the bias without attacking the individual—it should come across that it's their speech or behavior that's problematic, not a flaw with their character or personality. Similarly, you should consider both your boss' personality and the reaction of those around you if the bias arises in a public setting like a meeting or other group discussion. If the leader has a demonstrated history of valuing inclusivity, or if others in the room are visibly bothered, it may be productive to question the bias in the moment; otherwise, a private conversation after the fact will often be received better.

Whether you bring it up in the moment or wait, preparing phrases to start and end the talk can help it feel less awkward and prevent an emotional back-and-forth. Draw the leader's attention to what they said and why it bothered you, then give them a chance to own and apologize for their comment. Like in other situations, asking questions is often better than accusatory statements. A great question could be something like, "The way you phrased that could be taken the wrong way. Could you explain exactly what you meant?" This brings attention to the bias but implies any offense was unintentional, giving the speaker the benefit of the doubt. Another option is to phrase it from your perspective, something like, "[Word/phrase/action] isn't okay with me because [reason], and I would appreciate it if you avoided that kind of language/behavior in the future." Avoid loaded words like racism, sexism, and homophobia, which can be automatic fight-or-flight triggers. As an example, say your manager doesn't want to promote a black colleague because they wear their hair in braids and the boss sees this as "unprofessional." It would be accurate to describe this thought process as racist, but doing so likely won't help anyone. Instead, you could point out that they're the most qualified individual, or ask if a white colleague's hairstyle affected their promotion decision. These accomplish the same goal of making the person double-check their decision-making without as much risk they'll go into defense mode and shut down the conversation.

The use of subjective language to describe member performance is a common form of marginalization and discrimination. These could be blanket statements with little actual meaning (e.g. someone's "not a good cultural fit") or coded phrases, like calling someone "difficult" or "challenging to manage." In other cases, traits that would be seen as positive in the majority are described as negatives for minority communities. A white male is a "go-getter" who's "refreshingly straightforward"; a black woman is "too direct" or "not a team player" when they act the exact same way. Questioning these subjective phrases encourages gatekeepers to examine their double-standards and can prompt further self-analysis of their own biases, and can be an effective non-confrontational way to raise awareness of bias in organization leaders. Remember that discrimination doesn't always manifest as hateful words or actions. In some cases, it could come through as avoidance or discomfort, and this can be just as damaging for members' progress if it means the boss has a stronger rapport with male employees than female ones, or with white employees than those from other races. Undoing these less aggressive forms of discrimination and bias is just as important as rooting out overt -isms when you want to give every member the same degree of psychological safety.

While the goals of calling out a superior's bias are the same as addressing it in peers and reports, the process can be more difficult. For one thing, it's more intimidating to stand up to someone who has power over you, especially if you're one of the few people (or the only person) from a certain background in the organization. If the boss has a history of toxic or discriminatory behavior, you may feel you're risking your career to confront them (and may be right). A deeply biased boss may attack you for confronting them rather than acknowledging your concern, or start thinking of you as one of those "difficult" employees left out of consideration for promotions and high-level projects. Again, it all depends on the boss. If they're generally fair and care about their team's well-being, they may be unaware of how biases impact their thoughts and appreciate your willingness to point them out. If they've shown resistance to inclusion efforts in the past, or you're not sure how the boss feels about diversity, the conversation warrants a bit more caution.

Talking to a trusted ally about your observations and concerns is a good first step. Ask your colleagues about their experiences with the leader in question and observe the leader's interactions with others. This can help clarify the specific issues or biases at work and allows you to gather more examples, beyond your personal experience, that you can cite during a future conversation. Along with this, keep a personal record of your negative experiences or discrimination you've observed. This documentation will be useful if the leader asks for proof of their poor behavior, or if you need to file an official report down the road. In a larger organization with multiple leaders, it may be helpful to take your concerns to another supervisor and ask them to address the issue—critical feedback from a peer may be less likely to get a defensive response than that same feedback from a subordinate.

Something else to keep in mind: it's not your responsibility to fix your bosses or organization, especially if you're doing so at the cost of your own mental health or career security. It's most important to speak up if the biased leadership is directly impacting your career progress or causing stress in your daily work environment. When the biased leader has no direct impact on your workday, consider your own psychological safety along with that of your colleagues when deciding how to address the situation. If you don't feel comfortable having a face-to-face conversation with the boss, a letter or e-mail can be a great alternative. Not only does this let you express your concerns without direct confrontation, but it also creates a written record of the discriminatory behavior that you can include in an official report, should the situation escalate to that point. If the leader continues to act on biases, or takes retribution against you for raising the issue, it's time to go to the next step: either HR or the boss' boss, depending on the structure of your organization.

IDENTIFYING STRUCTURAL BIASES

While an individual's motivations aren't always crystal clear from their words and actions, they're often still easier to address than biases that have been worked into an organization's policies and other structures. The barriers to change are often different, too. You may have full support from the leadership team and an over-arching desire for more inclusivity but lack the resources or time to re-write established policies.

Some common signs of bias at the institutional level include:

- Leadership and gatekeeper positions are held predominantly or exclusively by members of the dominant group.
- Standards and expectations are assumed or unspoken, rather than clearly defined.
- Promotions and accolades are given based on unearned privilege rather than observable behavior and accomplishments.
- The work environment and policies favor the dominant group, or are written solely from the dominant group's perspective.
- The organization's core values aren't reflected in the culture and work environment.

Of course, many of these can be signs of other types of toxicity and dysfunctionality. So how can you identify when bias is the problem? The best way is to get input from more voices on the fairness and effectiveness of organization policies. Employee surveys can be a great tool for gauging individuals' feelings of belonging. Don't ask questions about the organization's diversity, but instead focus on their experience within it, like whether they feel respected, whether their opinion is valued, and how they'd be treated by management in an ideal workplace.

The issue with employee surveys is that they will only reflect the perspectives of members. If you're struggling with diversity, the voices of those affected by discriminatory policies may still not be heard. In this case, leadership needs to take a more scientific approach to the problem. Identify where in your process diversity is being impeded. Very often, this starts with auditing the hiring process. Review the wording of job descriptions and which talent pools you recruit from, paying particular attention to your referral process, a common source of new hires for many organizations. A small change, like switching to a blind review of applications, can prevent common biases like name bias from influencing the process. Standardizing the interview process can also be very helpful in this regard. Unstructured interviews are particularly likely to allow individual biases to influence the process, and have been proven a poorer predictor of job performance than data-driven assessments like skill tests. Make sure all candidates are asked the same questions during the interview process and create a measurable scoring rubric for hiring managers to use so that all applicants are considered according to the same standards.

As a general rule, the more objective the organization's decision-making processes, the lower the risk that bias will be able to influence them. When auditing your processes to root out sources of bias, let data inform these decisions. If the entire leadership is homogenous but lower organization levels are diverse, the data points toward some form of discrimination in the promotion process. Pay attention to pay disparities as well as promotion rates, and analyze how pay rates are determined if the data shows non-white or female members consistently earn less than their majority counterparts. Similarly, check your messaging against your reality. A company that says it embraces multi-culturalism should also demonstrate this in its membership and customer base. If it doesn't, take a closer look to figure out where that messaging is breaking down.

Organizations often take a reactive approach to increasing diversity, focusing on removing things that could be offensive or problematic. This is important work, but it's not the only approach that you can take. A more proactive strategy is to implement intentionally inclusive policies that institutionalize equity. How are these different? Consider the hypothetical of a company with a biased personal appearance policy that specifies white-centric hairstyles as the only acceptable options. A reactive response would be to add Afro-centric hairstyles to the approved list after a black employee raises concerns. A proactive response would be rephrasing the guideline to emphasize its core intent (maintaining professional grooming standards) without banning any specific hairstyles so the policy is more universally inclusive.

Simply setting diversity goals can be a challenge, much less figuring out how to achieve them. It's helpful to remember that measurable isn't synonymous with countable. Regular surveys gauging employees' feelings of belonging are an example of measurable non-numerical benchmarks related to inclusivity. The crucial components of a diversity goal that it have a defined timeline for achievement, a realistic and clearly stated goal, and a data-based metric for gauging progress and success.

THE BOTTOM LINE ON IDENTIFYING BIAS

Unexamined norms allow biases to perpetuate unchecked, whether they exist at the individual or the institutional level. Challenging and exposing these norms is the first step toward creating a more inclusive organization. The good news is, unconscious biases aren't permanent. They can take some time to break down, but even the most long-established bias can be removed, and the impact of these biases can be lessened by implementing policies that focus on facts and data over opinions and perceptions.

Unconscious bias negatively effects everyone in an organization, not only those who are its direct target. It breaks down trust when people see unfair decisions made, for one thing, and prevents some team members from contributing their full talents—and that only makes everyone's job harder. On the plus side, data shows those who feel able to speak up about bias have a higher sense of workplace satisfaction and belonging, and report less negativity toward those who express bias around them. In other words, once you start the work and make team members feel safe speaking up, you're already on the right path to a stronger, more inclusive team.

CHAPTER 10:

The Wheel of Inclusivity

While creating an inclusive culture can be a difficult task, inclusivity itself is not a complicated concept. At its heart, it means making your organization a place members feel like they belong and can be their true selves. To do that requires four key concepts: respect, awareness, intention, and transparency. You can think of these concepts as the four spokes of a wheel. All four are necessary for a stable inclusive culture, and your wheel of inclusivity may not last long if you're missing one of these key pillars. On the positive side, strengthening any one concept can improve the integrity of the entire culture, and when you want to move forward on diversity and equity initiatives, putting energy into any one of the four spokes can start the wheel turning.

What role does each of these concepts play in inclusivity—and how can you increase them in your organization? We'll tackle those questions in this chapter, going into each of these four concepts in more depth and providing some actionable strategies for improvement.

CONCEPT 1: RESPECT

In a 2015 report, the Society for Human Resource Management surveyed employees on their level of job satisfaction and the overall culture of their workplace. Respectful treatment of all employees was the top contributor to job satisfaction, followed by a culture of trust between management and employees—which is arguably another form of respect; trust forms when you believe the other person respects your identity, boundaries, and abilities. While it's nice to have data to confirm this, it's also basic common sense: people want to be part of a group where their perspective and skills are valued equally to everyone else's.

Respect is the foundation of ethical behavior and the basis of all human relationships. At its core, it means believing that a person has the right to not just exist but to have their voice heard and their unique contributions celebrated. Equity is respect in action, based in the fundamental belief that all individuals should have equal access to opportunities and taking steps to provide it to those at a disadvantage. A culture of mutual respect fosters greater diversity because employees feel comfortable sharing ideas and giving critical feedback, which in turn creates better, more inclusive policies that are less likely to be influenced by bias.

How do you foster this type of mutual respect in an organization? Here are some approaches:

Encourage cross-cultural sharing.

You can't respect someone's culture if you don't know what it is. Stereotypes and offensive behavior are often rooted in ignorance. The more you know about someone's background, values, and traditions, the less likely you'll be to say or do something that makes them uncomfortable—and that means they'll share more of their true selves, encouraging further cultural sharing and understanding.

Leaders can start this by setting the example, but anyone on the team can encourage more open conversation. A good first step is to get to know the people you work with beyond their job description. This doesn't mean prying into every detail of their personal life; mutual respect also means letting others have their privacy, and it's important to remember that personal boundaries differ on topics like family and religion. A great place to start the conversation is asking about their passions or interests, following up with questions or comments that show your genuine interest and build a rapport. In meetings, keep track of who speaks the most and actively prompt quieter members to share their perspective. An open dialogue that involves a variety of voices encourages more open sharing throughout the organization.

Revising or replacing outdated policies can also encourage more cultural sharing. For example, a strict dress code has a homogenizing effect on the team, and often creates inequity because some people have to alter their appearance more than others to conform. Relaxing these policies increases cultural sharing in two ways. First, it lets people show more of their individuality, increasing other team members' exposure to attire, jewelry, or hair styles they may have stereotypical associations with. Just as important, it lessens the feeling among team members that they have to hide parts of themselves to fit in, which can make them more likely to share other parts of themselves, too.

Be a better listener.

In a productive conversation, all parties feel like they're able to contribute and are heard when they speak. Interrupting or talking over people sends the message your words are more important than theirs; similarly, if you're distracted or doing other things, the speaker feels like those things matter more to you than what they're saying.

Nobody likes being ignored, or feeling like they're shouting into a void. If you want people to share more you need to listen to them when they do speak up. This means putting down the phone, turning away from the computer, and giving them your full attention—and, when they're talking, focusing on their words, not preparing the next thing you want to say. It also means remembering what was said after the conversation's over. This is especially crucial for managers and leaders when they get feedback from team members. If you make changes based on that feedback, follow up with the employee to let them know; if you can't, explain why, and work with them to find another solution to their problem if you're able. When leading meetings, ensure everyone in the room pays attention when their colleagues share, and coach members who are struggling in better active listening techniques.

Establish and maintain boundaries.

As we mentioned above, respecting others' right to privacy is an important part of an overall culture of respect. It should be up to each individual how much they want to share about their lives outside of the workplace. When someone asks a question that crosses their personal information boundaries, they should feel empowered to say that's a topic they'd rather not discuss, even if the person asking is their boss or another leader. It's important to normalize this as a response when you're working toward a more open workplace dialogue so that individuals are able to set comfortable boundaries.

Time boundaries are another crucial part of a respectful workplace. When team members show up late to meetings (or managers allow them to go an hour past their scheduled end time) this sends a message to everyone else that their time isn't important. Managers should be especially conscious of this when they're scheduling and communicating with team members. Work calls during free time, ignoring time off requests, or changing schedules on short notice is disrespectful of the employee's work/life balance, and gives the impression you only care about their job role, not their life and self-outside the workplace.

Make event planning collaborative.

Team building events and traditions in organizations are often derived from the majority culture—and they likely will continue to be, if the only people involved in their planning are part of that majority. Even organizations actively increasing diversity in other areas often neglect the more social aspect of the workplace, but that's an easy place to generate more cultural understanding and not something that should be ignored. The next time you're planning a team outing or workplace celebration, ask for input from the people who aren't normally involved. If you have international team members, find out what celebrations happen in their country and do your own version.

Improve conflict resolution policies.

Conflict is an unfortunate inevitability any time you're dealing with a group of people. The more diverse and multi-cultural your organization, the higher the risk of misunderstandings and personality clashes. A respectful workplace doesn't mean one that's free of conflict, but one in which conflicts are addressed promptly and fairly. A comprehensive conflict resolution process should include both confidential reporting and peer-to-peer mediation options. It should also specify how complaints of harassment, discrimination, or bullying are addressed, both between peers and in employee/manager relationships.

CONCEPT 2: AWARENESS

Education is one of your best tools for fighting bias and increasing inclusivity. The more your team knows about unconscious biases and other forms of discrimination, the better they'll be able to spot them in the wild—both in the actions of others and in their own thought processes. Training employees how to slow down and interrogate their decision making gives them the tools they need to mitigate the impacts of bias, not just in the workplace but in their day-to-day lives.

There's another side to awareness, too, and it overlaps in many places with what we talked about in the previous section on respect. When team members are more aware of the many cultures and backgrounds represented in the organization, they're better able to avoid making unintentionally offensive remarks. The more exposure someone has to a particular group, the less likely they'll be to rely on stereotypes to form opinions and make decisions. This is why cultural education is as important as bias training when your goal is true inclusivity.

Before you can increase awareness in your organization, it's often necessary to push back against denial. Nobody wants to think of themselves as biased. Even those who are fully aware of how unconscious biases form may be blind to their own and the extent of their influence; in fact, these individuals may be the ones to resist the most when asked to go through unconscious bias training or other education programs. Presenting data that demonstrates the need for more bias awareness can help to break down this argument, but it often still requires persistence to shift the culture to one where people are encouraged to share their biases and point out those they see in others.

Once you get buy-in from your team that more bias awareness is needed, the next step is finding the right kind of education for your team. Here is some advice on choosing and implementing anti-bias education:

Choose a training that gives participants strategies for reducing bias.

Not all anti-bias training is equal in its effectiveness. A poorly-run training can actually have the opposite effect, making people feel like they're supporting diversity even though they haven't made any real effort to do so. As a result, they perpetuate biases at the same time they're patting themselves on the back for being so inclusive.

The goal of an effective anti-bias training is for participants to leave, not just with knowledge of biases, but also with tools and strategies to identify and reduce it. Some of the best implement prejudice habit-breaking practice, guiding participants through the steps of breaking down a bias so they can see the process in action. Highlight common forms of bias is a great first step, but it's better if they're paired with examples of how to undo them. Effective training also goes deeper than the current bias, encouraging participants to explore its roots so they can understand how it formed in the first place.

Provide ongoing education.

There is no one-stop solution to bias. Just like diversity and inclusivity as a whole, eliminating bias from decision making is an ongoing process. Scheduling regular anti-bias training ensures new hires can get those same skills and tools as established team members, and lets older employees get a refresher. This kind of recurring training also sends the message that you're serious about undoing biases and committed to the work involved.

Combined with these formal trainings, make sure employees have a chance to live what they've learned. If someone calls out a microaggression during a meeting, for example, don't gloss over it; use this as an opportunity to collectively practice your bias-busting strategies.

Pair this with cultural education that increases team member awareness of varying perspectives and backgrounds. Making these cultural events fun and social turns them into morale-builders, as well, and can help shift diversity training from a "have to" to a "want to" for your team.

Follow through with data and accountability.

Any time you implement a new process in an organization, you want to make sure it's working the way you intended. Employee pulse surveys are a helpful way to track the team's feelings of belonging and identify ways you can improve or refine your inclusivity efforts. Along with this, keep your eye on other data, like leadership diversity, team member pay, and turnover demographics, which can be key indicators of an organization's overall inclusivity.

Another crucial aspect of diversity training is showing members what is and is not okay within the organization. This is where accountability comes into play. Once someone has completed anti-bias training, don't let ignorance be an excuse for biased behavior or microaggressions. Leaders should be proactive in addressing potential bias when they observe it and encourage team members to do the same. This should start with conversation that helps the offending individual understand the error of their ways, but may need to involve disciplinary action if they refuse to adjust their behavior, especially if they're in a gatekeeper position and could negatively impact your efforts toward inclusion.

CONCEPT 3: INTENTION

Like the other concepts on the wheel, intention exists at both the individual and organizational level. For individuals, intentional decision making happens when you take the time to examine the rationale behind your thought process, and have the self-awareness to realize when you're missing a key perspective. At the organizational level, intention means committing to inclusivity in your actions, culture, and interactions with customers or clients—not relegating it to a slogan on your website or an afterthought addition to your employee handbook.

We've already outlined some ways for individuals to be more intentional with their thought process, and that same advice applies. Here are other strategies you can take to lead with intent when it comes to diversity, both on the individual and organizational level.

Infuse diversity into every aspect of the organization.

In many organizations, diversity is treated as a discrete entity, and this is a factor in why diversity initiatives often fail to significantly move the needle. When diversity is seen as the responsibility of a select few, it comes into play after key decisions are already made, and by then the damage has often already been done. Conversely, making diversity a core value makes it everybody's responsibility, encouraging decision makers in all departments and levels to think about diversity on a day-to-day basis.

Writing diversity into your mission statement and policies shows that it's something you're fully committed to as an organization, and makes it more likely you'll see real change in the culture. Consider every department and process through an inclusivity lens. This includes both internal departments, like HR and management, and public-facing areas like marketing and customer support. Taking a holistic approach to inclusivity helps keep your messaging consistent and get full buy-in from the entire team.

Set and communicate inclusivity goals.

An effective goal is measurable, achievable, and specific in its aims and methods, with a defined deadline. This doesn't change with goals related to DEI. Your ultimate goal can be a more inclusive organization, but to achieve that you'll need to set smaller milestones along the way, targeting the specific areas where your team is lacking.

This starts with identifying what diversity goals will have the most value for your organization. Collect feedback from team members, especially those in under-represented groups, and find out what changes they want to see. Combine this with data on your hiring, promotions, compensation, and turnover to pinpoint where your efforts will have the most impact. Once the goals are set, communicate them clearly to every member of the organization. This should include sharing why this goal is important, what steps you'll be taking to get there, when you expect to see results, and what you hope to achieve.

Actively seek missing perspectives.

It's not enough to throw a line about diversity onto your job description then post it in the same places you sourced your current homogenous team. Actively seeking diversity means identifying which communities aren't represented then putting in the work to find out what they want in an organization (and, just as important, what bothers them or triggers as a red flag). You also need to meet them where they are by reaching out through the right institutions and networks.

This advice doesn't only apply to recruiting, either. Leaders who assign team members to projects or choose meeting participants should ask themselves what perspectives are missing before finalizing the roster. Take a look back at previous invite lists or team assignments, too, and look for patterns or notable omissions that you can correct moving forward.

On an individual level, consider your professional network. The next time you open LinkedIn or another social media page, scroll through your contacts list. Do those people all look the same—and do most of them look like you? If so, that's a likely sign your network is fairly insular. Luckily, these platforms also make it easy to expand your network with a bit of intentional searching. If you prefer in-person networking, professional organizations are a great way to start. Along with all-purpose resource groups, many industries have dedicated organizations for professionals from marginalized communities. Reach out to a local chapter and ask if you can attend their next event, then follow up with the people you meet to show you have a genuine interest in forming a professional connection.

Give critiques full consideration.

Even the best-intentioned organization is likely to make some missteps on the road toward inclusivity. When someone calls you out on it, listen to their feedback and resist the temptation to argue or defend, even if the criticism seems unjustified from your perspective. This is true of comments from outside as well as within the organization. If you get a customer complaint of racist treatment, talk with the individuals involved to get each person's perspective on what happened and identify what went wrong and why. Similarly, if a coworker tells you something you did offended them, apologize and find out why it was a problem and what would be better to say or do in the future.

You can explain that the offense was accidental as part of this conversation, but that shouldn't come in lieu of an apology. Think of it this way: if you're playing catch and accidentally throw a ball through a window, the glass is just as broken as if you threw it through on purpose. The same is true of words. You didn't mean to offend, but the hurt the other person feels is real.

CONCEPT 4: TRANSPARENCY

In a transparent workplace, the lines of communication are open between levels of the hierarchy. Leaders know what's happening at the member level and listen to their feedback; members know their expectations and how well they're meeting them, and are given access to information and resources. This free flow of information leaves fewer blind spots for biases to go unchecked and welcomes a multitude of perspectives into discussions.

Transparency and privacy might seem to contradict, but a healthy workplace has both in the right balance. The first test for whether information should be shared is that it be relevant. If a coworker tells you personal information in confidence, you shouldn't share that in the name of transparency; that's non-work information, and it's their right to choose who they share with. The second test is whether sharing it could cause direct harm. Proprietary recipes or formulas can be kept secret even in a transparent workplace, for example, since revealing them could hurt the company's competitive advantage. Sensitive financial data also often needs to be kept private, though that shouldn't be used as an excuse to hide overall revenue numbers from employees—if it's something you'd share with a stockholder, transparency says it should be available to everyone in the organization.

Managers and leaders have the most agency for increasing transparency. Transparent leaders share information that could be useful to their teams. When you're wrong or don't know an answer, admit it and let your reports make suggestions. Invite input into your decision-making and explain the how and why behind your decisions when you're able. Some other strategies you can use to increase transparency:

Standardize communication and collaboration platforms.

This is especially important as organizations shift to remote and hybrid formats, when there's no backup in-person option for people to get information. If you don't have one already, add a section on communication into your employee handbook that details where, how, and how often team members should communicate with coworkers, managers, and clients. Using a project management tool or CRM can be a great way to increase transparency, too, bringing all your communication together in one place and making it easy for team members to share thoughts and feedback.

Open communication with management and HR is another important piece of this puzzle. If an employee wants to file a complaint or make a suggestion, they should know exactly what to do and who to send it to. The same is true of requesting days off, signing up for professional development or networking events, or taking advantage of other workplace benefits.

It's also important that you cut off any "back door" communication channels. An example of this is employees texting requests off to a manager's personal phone rather than going through the official call-off system. This leads to confusion if the information doesn't get passed along correctly. It can also create inequity; the manager sees the requests from the people with their number first, and could give it preference over a request from an employee who's not in their inner circle and went through the correct channels.

Give everyone easy access to resources and information.

The best way to do this is to create a central, dedicated area where team members know they can go to access the handbook, operating procedures, training manuals, and any other resources that can help them do their jobs. This can be a physical space in an office or a virtual shared drive, as long as everybody can access it.

Another part of this is being transparent with the responsibilities and expectations for members. Don't just rattle them off at orientation; follow up with members to make sure they fully understand, and provide correcting feedback when they don't live up to them. Managers can help by having more frequent check-ins with reports and making themselves available to answer questions when they have them.

Share news and results.

Often, employees get a lot of updates on projects while they're in progress but don't hear whether their work was successful. Keep the whole team in the loop on all stages of their work, even after it's left their hands. Sharing results helps team members know what works and what doesn't. When it's a success, congratulate the team and acknowledge their hard work. When projects fail, share that, too, and use the opportunity to refine your process and correct mistakes.

This applies on the big-picture level, too. When you release quarterly reports, include members on the list of people it goes out to (or add it to the shared resource area you've created). If the company's facing a setback or scandal, let the whole team know what's going on. Sharing news that could affect the company shows that you see them as crucial parts of the team and will prevent rumors from spreading that could add further confusion.

PUTTING THE WHEEL IN MOTION

Now that you know how respect, awareness, intention, and transparency build an inclusive culture, it's time to put what you've learned into action. Use the inclusivity scoresheet to gauge which of these areas is the weakest in your organization. The questions that follow it can help you get better feedback from team members, while the worksheet will help you set DEI goals.

INCLUSIVITY SCORESHEET

Read each of the statements below, then score it based on the following scale:

- 0 = Never true in my organization
- 1 = Sometimes/partially true in my organization
- 2 = Always true in my organization

The area with the lowest score is the one you should focus on first, but a score of 5 or lower in any of the concepts indicates it's a serious impediment to inclusivity, and an area you should target for improvement.

Respect

1. Members are encouraged to share their background and culture with colleagues.
2. Leadership solicits feedback from members and acts on the information they receive.
3. Employees are empowered to set and maintain boundaries.
4. We have an effective, confidential conflict resolution system.
5. Workplace celebrations and social activities are based on a variety of cultural traditions.

6. There is a high level of trust between members and leadership.
7. The unique individuality of members is appreciated and celebrated.

Awareness

1. We offer training in unconscious bias mitigation to members.
2. Members are given skills and tools to identify bias in themselves and others.
3. Members are encouraged to call out bias in the workplace.
4. Employees feel safe pointing out bias in leaders or managers.
5. Inclusivity is tracked and measured.
6. Members are held accountable for their words and actions.
7. Members have the opportunity to interact with a variety of people and cultures.

Intention

1. Diversity is included in our mission statement and core values.
2. Our messaging on diversity is consistent through the organization.
3. We set specific, measurable inclusivity goals.
4. DEI goals get full support and commitment from all levels of the organization.
5. Reports of bias or discrimination are taken seriously, regardless of their source.
6. We review and revise our policies to make them more inclusive.
7. Diversity is a factor in the decision making process at all levels.

Transparency

1. All members use the same communication and collaboration platforms.
2. Members are able to share feedback with leadership.
3. Member responsibilities and expectations are clearly communicated.
4. Information and resources are easy for all members to access.
5. Managers and leaders involve other perspectives in their decision making process.
6. Managers explain their decision-making process to reports. Major news and company information is shared with employees.

20 EMPLOYEE PULSE QUESTIONS FOR INCLUSIVITY

1. How often do you feel excited by or passionate about the work you do here?
2. Do you feel that your work is valued by management and leadership?
3. Do you feel you have adequate opportunities to develop and learn new skills?
4. Can you see yourself growing your career with this company?
5. Do you feel there are clear, concrete steps you could take to advance within the organization?
6. Do you feel supported by your managers?
7. Do you feel that you're held to the same standards as your colleagues?
8. Do you feel you can identify with members of the executive board or upper leadership?
9. Have you received or been offered mentorship during your time with the company?

10. Do you have all the tools and resources you need to do your job effectively?

11. Do you feel like the company is aligned with your core values?

12. Do you feel that you're able to be your true, full self in the workplace?

13. Do you feel that your colleagues respect and value your opinions?

14. Does the workplace environment allow you to do your best work?

15. Do you feel empowered to share ideas, suggestions, and other feedbacks with your colleagues?

16. Do you have someone in the workplace you feel you can trust and confide in?

17. If you experienced harassment or bullying in the workplace, would you feel safe reporting it to HR or management?

18. Have you experienced bias during your time with the company? If so, was it addressed?

19. Would you refer a friend to this company?

20. Do you feel proud to work for this company?

DEI GOAL SETTING WORKSHEET

Our goal is _________________________________. We will know we've achieved this goal when _________________________________, and we intend to achieve it by ___/_____/___.

The steps we'll take to achieve this goal are:

____

____

____

____

We'll track the following metrics to evaluate our progress:

____

____

____

____

The specific need or issue we hope to address by achieving this goal is:

____

____

____

____

The main obstacles to achieving this goal are:

____

____

____

____

RESEARCH SOURCES AND WORKS CITED

"10 Benefits of Diversity in the Workplace." *Washington State University Carson College of Business Blog,* 14 January 2021, https://onlinemba.wsu.edu/blog/10-benefits-of-diversity-in-the-workplace/.

"64% of Consumers Consider Making an Immediate Purchase After Seeing Diverse Advertisements, New Data Shows." *Cision PR Newswire,* 11 November 2020, https://www.prnewswire.com/news-releases/64-of-consumers-consider-making-an-immediate-purchase-after-seeing-diverse-advertisements-new-data-shows-301170981.html.

"8 Essential Traits of an Inclusive Workplace." *Limeade Institute Blog,* 2 February 2020, https://www.limeade.com/resources/blog/inclusive-workplace/.

Apfelbaum, Evan. "The Trouble With Homogenous Teams." *MIT Sloan Management Review Magazine Vol. 59 No. 2,* winter 2018.

Barnum, Matt. "Race, not just poverty, shapes who graduates in America – and other education lessons from a big new study." *Chalkbeat*, 23 March 2018, https://www.chalkbeat.org/2018/3/23/21104601/.

"Barriers and benefits of diversity in the workplace." *Western Governors University*, 4 June 2019, https://www.wgu.edu/blog/barriers-benefits-diversity-workplace1906.html#close.

Bersin, Josh. "Why Diversity and Inclusion Has Become a Business Priority." *The Josh Bersin Company*, 7 December 2015, https://joshbersin.com/2015/12/why-diversity-and-inclusion-will-be-a-top-priority-for-2016/.

Broady, Kristen and Brad Hershbein. "Major decisions: What graduates earn over their lifetimes." *The Brookings Institute*, 8 October 2020, https://www.brookings.edu/blog/up-front/2020/10/08/major-decisions-what-graduates-earn-over-their-lifetimes/.

Caprino, Kathy. "New Data Reveals the Hard Costs of Bias and How to Disrupt It." *Forbes*, 26 October 2017, https://www.forbes.com/sites/kathycaprino/2017/10/26/new-data-reveals-the-hard-costs-of-bias-and-how-to-disrupt-it/?sh=4131c5d74595.

Chetty, Raj et. al. "Race and Economic Opportunity in the United States: An Intergenerational Perspective." *The Equality of Opportunity Project*, March 2018.

Coffman, Katherine and Francesca Gino. "Unconscious Bias Training That Works." *Harvard Business Review Magazine*, September-October 2021.

Darling-Hammond, Linda. "Unequal Opportunity: Race and Education." *The Brookings Institute*, 1 March 1998, https://www.brookings.edu/articles/unequal-opportunity-race-and-education/.

Dayton, Denise. "Examples of Equal Opportunities Within the Workplace." *Chron*, 23 March 2021, https://work.chron.com/examples-equal-opportunities-within-workplace-14551.html.

Diaz Mejias, Ashley and Tiffany Jana. "Erasing Institutional Bias: Structural Change, Starting with You." *Porchlight Books blog*, 14 November 2018,
https://www.porchlightbooks.com/blog/changethis/2018/erasing-institutional-bias-structural-change-starting-with-you.

Dowd, Mary. "How to Deal With a Biased Boss." *Chron*, 7 July 2020, https://work.chron.com/deal-biased-boss-4501.html.

"Easing Racial Tensions at Work." *Coqual*, https://coqual.org/reports/easing-racial-tensions-at-work/.

Elue, Chinasa. "The Impact of Microaggressions on Health and Job Satisfaction." *Southern Regional Education Board blog*, 1 December 2020,
https://www.sreb.org/blog-post/impact-microaggressions-health-and-job-satisfaction.

Etheridge, Neslie A. "Effects of discrimination in the workplace." *U.S. Army CECOM Equal Employment Opportunity Office*, 12 February 2015, https://www.army.mil/article/142799/.

Fast Company Executive Board. "12 ways to consider different perspectives before making an important business decision." *Fast Company blog*, 16 March 2021,
https://www.fastcompany.com/90613258/.

Forbes Councils Member Expert Panel. "14 Important Benefits of a More Diverse Leadership Team." *Forbes.com*, 24 June 2021,
https://www.forbes.com/sites/forbescoachescouncil/2021/06/24/14-important-benefits-of-a-more-diverse-leadership-team/?sh =388f462f1f9b.

Francis, Dania and Christian E. Weller. "The Black-White Wealth

Gap Will Widen Educational Disparities During the Coronavirus Pandemic." *Center for American Progress*, 12 August 2020, https://www.americanprogress.org/article/black-white-wealth-gap-will-widen-educational-disparities-coronavirus-pandemic/.

Gassam Asare, Janice. "Your Unconscious Bias Trainings Keep Failing Because You're Not Addressing Systemic Bias." *Forbes*, 29 December 2019, https://www.forbes.com/sites/janicegassam/2020/12/29/your-unconscious-bias-trainings-keep-failing-because-youre-not-addressing-systemic-bias/?sh=3ea299691e9d.

Goodman, Rachel. "Why Amazon's Automated Hiring Tool Discriminated Against Women." *ACLU Blog*, 12 October 2018, https://www.aclu.org/blog/womens-rights/womens-rights-workplace/why-amazons-automated-hiring-tool-discriminated-against.

Hewlett, Sylvia Ann, Melinda Marshall, and Laura Sherbin. "How Diversity Can Drive Innovation." *Harvard Business Review*, December 2013.

Hewlett, Sylvia Ann, Ripa Rashid, and Laura Sherbin. "When Employees Think the Boss Is Unfair, They're More Likely to Disengage and Leave." *Harvard Business Review*, 1 August 2017, https://hbr.org/2017/08/when-employees-think-the-boss-is-unfair-theyre-more-likely-to-disengage-and-leave.

Hilliard, Brian. "Be Intentional About Diversity." *Entrepreneur.com*, 10 August 2020, https://www.entrepreneur.com/article/354300.

Holder, Natalie. "The Top Five Barriers to Inclusion and Why You Should Avoid Them." *ASAE Center*, 30 January 2017, https://www.asaecenter.org/resources/articles/an_plus/2017/

january/the-top-five-barriers-to-inclusion-and-why-you-should-avoid-them.

Krentz, Matt. "Survey: What Diversity and Inclusion Policies Do Employees Actually Want?" *Harvard Business Review*, 5 February 2019, https://hbr.org/2019/02/survey-what-diversity-and-inclusion-policies-do-employees-actually-want.

Lagace, Martha. "How to Build a Fearless Organization." *Harvard Business School Working Knowledge*, 26 November 2018, https://hbswk.hbs.edu/item/make-your-employees-psychologically-safe.

Manyika, James, Jake Silberg, and Brittany Presten. "What Do We Do About the Biases in AI?" *Harvard Business Review*, 25 October 2019, https://hbr.org/2019/10/what-do-we-do-about-the-biases-in-ai.

Martin, Michael. "Poll: Majority of Americans Say Racial Discrimination Is A 'Big Problem'." *All Things Considered*, 21 June 2020.

McIntosh, Kriston, et. al. "Examining the Black-white wealth gap." *The Brookings Institute*, 27 February 2020, https://www.brookings.edu/blog/up-front/2020/02/27/examining-the-black-white-wealth-gap/.

McMullen, Troy. "The 'heartbreaking' decrease in black homeownership." *The Washington Post*, 28 February 2019.

Moreau, Elise. "How Unconscious Bias Can Impact the Workplace and Job Search." *The Balance Careers*, 16 November 2020, https://www.thebalancecareers.com/how-unconscious-bias-can-impact-the-workplace-and-job-search-5087838.

Morgan Roberts, Laura and Anthony J. Mayo. "Toward a Racially Just Workplace." *Harvard Business Review Big Idea Series: Advancing Black Leaders*, 14 November 2019, https://hbr.org/2019/11/toward-a-racially-just-workplace.

Murray, Seb. "Race and Leadership: The Black Experience in the Workplace." *University of Virginia Darden Ideas to Action*, 17 December 2019, https://ideas.darden.virginia.edu/race-and-leadership.

Nordell, Jessica. "Is This How Discrimination Ends?" *The Atlantic*, 7 May 2017, https://www.theatlantic.com/science/archive/2017/05/unconscious-bias-training/525405/.

Parakala, Kumar. "How To Overcome Barriers To Inclusion and Diversity." *Forbes Technology Council*, 17 June 2021, https://www.forbes.com/sites/forbestechcouncil/2021/06/17/how-to-overcome-barriers-to-inclusion-and-diversity/?sh=651bf3d16075.

Patel, Sujan. "10 Examples of Companies with Fantastic Cultures." *Entrepreneur*, 6 August 2015.

Przystanski, Andy. "How to Set Diversity and Inclusion Goals." *Lattice*, 28 January 2020, https://lattice.com/library/how-to-set-diversity-and-inclusion-goals.

Purbasari Horton, Anisa. "How to confront bias without alienating people." *Fast Company*, 18 April 2019, https://www.fastcompany.com/90333864/.

Rattan, Aneeta. "Your Boss Made a Biased Remark. Should You Confront Them?" *Harvard Business Review*, 22 December 2020, https://hbr.org/2020/12/your-boss-made-a-biased-remark-should-you-confront-them.

Reynolds, Katie. "13 benefits and challenges of cultural diversity in the workplace." *Hult International Business School Blog*, 17 January 2019, https://www.hult.edu/blog/benefits-challenges-cultural-diversity-workplace/.

Richeson, Jennifer A. and Richard J. Nussbaum. "The impact of multiculturalism versus color-blindness on racial bias." *Journal of Experimental Social Psychology 40*, 2004.

Sarkis, Stephanie. "Let's Talk About Racial Microaggressions In The Workplace." *Forbes*, 15 June 2020, https://www.forbes.com/sites/stephaniesarkis/2020/06/15/lets-talk-about-racial-microaggressions-in-the-workplace/?sh=749d03435d28.

Saska, Sarah. "How to define diversity, equity, and inclusion at work." *Culture Amp*, 5 November 2019, https://www.cultureamp.com/blog/diversity-equity-inclusion-work.

Suttie, Jill. "Three Ways Mindfulness Can Make You Less Biased." *Greater Good Magazine*, 15 May 2017, https://greatergood.berkeley.edu/article/item/three_ways_mindfulness_can_make_you_less_biased.

Torres, Monica. "These Coded Words Reveal Bosses Biases Against Certain Employees." 18 August 2020, https://www.huffpost.com/entry/subjective-words-boss-employee-bias_l_5f2aef71c5b64d7a55eda4fc.

Treseder, Dara. "Diversity Isn't a Checkbox: Here's How to Make It an Intentional Movement." *Business.com*, 16 September 2019.

"Understanding and Developing Organizational Culture." *The Society for Human Resource Management*, https://www.shrm.org/ResourcesAndTools/tools-and samples/toolkits/Pages/default.aspx.

Watkins, Michael D. "What Is Organizational Culture? And Why Should We Care?" *Harvard Business Review*, 15 May 2013.

Williams, Amber Lee. "How to Speak Up If You See Bias at Work." *Harvard Business Review*, 20 January 2017.

Wing Sue, Derald et. al. "Racial Microaggressions in Everyday Life." *American Psychologist Vol. 62 No. 4*, May-June 2007.

Yearby, Ruqaiijah. "The Impact of Structural Racism in Employment and Wages on Minority Women's Health." *Human Rights Magazine Vol. 43 No. 3: The State of Healthcare in the United States*, 2017.

Youmans, Sharon and Elizabeth Ozer. "Strategies to Address Unconscious Bias." *University of California, San Francisco Office of Diversity and Outreach*, https://diversity.ucsf.edu/resources/strategies-address-unconscious-bias.

Yuan, Karen. "Working While Black: Stories from black corporate America." *Fortune*, 16 June 2020, https://fortune.com/longform/working-while-black-in-corporate-america-racism-microaggressions-stories/.

RESOURCES AND FURTHER READING

ONLINE RESOURCES

50 Ways to Fight Bias

https://leanin.org/50-ways-to-fight-gender-bias

This free digital program through LeanIn.org has activities and resources for organizations of all sizes to identify and fight bias.

The Center for Association Leadership

https://www.asaecenter.org/resources/topics/diversity-and-inclusion

ASAE is a professional organization for managers and leaders, and their online resources are available to non-members. Their Diversity & Inclusion page has a robust collection of articles and information addressing a variety of specific DEI topics.

The Community Tool Box

https://ctb.ku.edu/en/table-of-contents

Curated by the Center for Community Health and Development at the University of Kansas, this site has information and resources to help organizations better meet the needs of their members, with sections focused on strategic planning, leadership, analyzing problems, and cultural competence.

The Society of Human Resource Management (SHRM) Toolkits
https://www.shrm.org/ResourcesAndTools/tools-and-samples/tool-kits/Pages/default.aspx
SHRM is one of the largest professional organizations focused on HR. The articles and resources on their website cover a range of HR topics, including helpful information, studies, and strategies related to diversity and inclusion.

FURTHER READING

Erasing Institutional Bias: How to Create Systemic Change for Organizational Inclusion, by Tiffany Jana, Jay Coen Gilbert, and Ashley Diaz Mejias (Berrett-Koehler Publishers, 2018)

The Fearless Organization: Creating Psychological Safety in the Workplace for Learning, Innovation, and Growth, by Amy C. Edmondson (John Wiley & Sons, Inc. 2019)

Inclusion: Diversity, the New Workplace & the Will to Change, by Jennifer Brown (Publish Your Purpose Press, 2017)

Race, Work, and Leadership: New Perspectives on the Black Experience, edited by Laura Morgan Roberts, Anthony J. Mayo, and David A. Thomas (Harvard Business School Publishing Corporation, 2019)

www.ingramcontent.com/pod-product-compliance
Lightning Source LLC
Chambersburg PA
CBHW050917260726
48660CB00001B/259